Optimal Language Learning

Optimal Language Learning

The Strategies and Epiphanies of Gifted Language Learners

Noumane Rahouti
and
Lawrence Baines

ROWMAN & LITTLEFIELD
Lanham • Boulder • New York • London

Published by Rowman & Littlefield
A wholly owned subsidiary of The Rowman & Littlefield Publishing Group, Inc.
4501 Forbes Boulevard, Suite 200, Lanham, Maryland 20706
www.rowman.com

Unit A, Whitacre Mews, 26-34 Stannary Street, London SE11 4AB

Copyright © 2017 by Noumane Rahouti and Lawrence Baines

All rights reserved. No part of this book may be reproduced in any form or by any electronic or mechanical means, including information storage and retrieval systems, without written permission from the publisher, except by a reviewer who may quote passages in a review.

British Library Cataloguing in Publication Information Available

Library of Congress Cataloging-in-Publication Data Available

ISBN: 978-1-4758-3388-1 (cloth : alk. papaer)
ISBN: 978-1-4758-3389-8 (pbk. : alk. paper)
ISBN: 978-1-4758-3390-4 (electronic)

∞™ The paper used in this publication meets the minimum requirements of American National Standard for Information Sciences—Permanence of Paper for Printed Library Materials, ANSI/NISO Z39.48-1992.

Printed in the United States of America

Contents

Acknowledgements	ix
Introduction to Optimal Language Learning	xi
1 Learning and Psycholinguistics	1
Knowledge of Languages As An Asset	2
2 The Quality of the Experience	5
Consciousness	5
Growth of the Self	6
Clear Goals and Feedback	8
The Autotelic Experience	9
Games	10
Obstacles	13
Body in Flow	13
Thought	14
Intrapersonal and Interpersonal Intelligence	15
Cheating Chaos	16
The Making of Meaning	17
3 Andrew	19
Interest in Languages	20
Moving to China	22
Functional Chinese	23
Language Epiphany	25
Photography	27
The Return	28
Analysis	29

4 Emmanuelle 33
Languages in School 34
Latin at Twelve 35
Spanish at Thirteen 36
Ancient Greek at Fifteen 37
English and Hebrew at Sixteen to Seventeen 37
Learning Language in Secondary School 38
Hungarian 39
More English, Lakota, and Italian in College 40
French in America 41
Teaching Non-American, Non–English-Speaking Students 43
Cherokee as A Graduate Student 43
Analysis 45

5 Rebecca 49
Childhood 49
College 51
Language Explosion 52
Spanish Fluency 54
Spanish Now 55
Analysis 56

6 Genevieve 61
Homseschooling 62
The Puzzle of Language 63
Arabic 64
France 66
Egypt 68
Analysis 69

7 Scott 71
Initial Encounters 72
Journeys 74
New Challenges 76
French 77
Crystallization 78
Perception of Languages 80
The Game 81
Analysis 82

Conclusions	85
1. The Environment is Critical	86
2. Periods of Intensive Study are Foundational	87
3. The Learner Should Exert Control Over the Experience	88
4. A Language Epiphany Will Come	90
5. The Urge to Merge is Natural and Beneficial	91
6. An Interest in Life Precedes an Interest in Language	92
7. There is No Single Path to Fluency	92
8. Flow is Subjective	93
9. Flow Amplifies Language Learning	95
References	97
About the Authors	103

Acknowledgements

Undertaking such a considerable work requires support, not only academic but emotional, interpersonal support. It requires the type of support that reminds you why you are doing, what you are doing, and why you should keep doing it. I dedicate this work to my parents who left their home country with the hope of offering their kids a better future. I also want to dedicate this work to Malika Rahouti and Chafik Rahouti, whose support was needed and tremendously helpful. I would like to thank Donna Alexander for being such a great inspiration throughout these years and Lawrence Baines for being such a great mentor. I also would like to thank Neil Houser, Sally Beach, and Courtney Vaughn for being such great teachers. Last but not least, I dedicate this work to Genevieve, Emma, Andrew, Rebecca, and Scott without whom none of this work would have been possible. I would like to thank them for opening up and sharing their exceptional life experiences.

—Noumane Rahouti

I want to thank Noumane for inviting me to work with him on this fascinating project. Also, thanks to Jean Oliver, Janet Gorton, Noreen Hanlon, Taewoong Kim, and Ed Farrell for their substantial help with early drafts of the book. As always, I am grateful to Coleen and Robert for putting up with me.

—Lawrence Baines

Introduction

Every year, a flurry of new books are published that promise to teach mastery of a foreign language in a relatively short time span. Consider some recent titles:

Fluent in 3 Months: How Anyone at Any Age Can Learn to Speak Any Language from Anywhere in the World (Lewis, 2014).
Fluent Forever: How to Learn Any Language Fast and Never Forget It (Wyner, 2014).
How to Learn Any Language in a Few Months While Enjoying Yourself: 45 Proven Tips for Language Learners (Nicholson, 2014).
How I Learned to Speak Spanish Fluently in Three Months: Discover How You Can Conquer Spanish Easily the Same (Oakfield, 2016).
How to Learn a Foreign Language in Four Months: Proven Methods for Fluency (Penn, 2016).

Most books that promise fast and easy second language acquisition are not based on research of any kind. Rather, they combine homilies about the importance of developing a positive attitude with a mandate to "really listen," and the vague assurance that the process toward fluency will be effortless. While it might be appealing to hear that language learning is easy, unfortunately, it is not. Despite the confident assurances of charlatans selling language books, there is no getting around the intense, complex work involved in becoming fluent in another language.

Of course, the audience for quick and easy bromides for language success may largely comprise people who have tried—and failed—to learn another language. Rather than base a language learning system on false promises of instantaneous fluency, *Optimal Language Learning* takes a different approach. *Optimal Language Learning* investigates the vast, (mostly) unbiased body of research on language acquisition in concert with close analyses of the techniques of individuals who have developed a remarkable affinity for becoming fluent in foreign languages.

The techniques of these *language mavens* are brought to light and thoroughly examined to demonstrate how real experts get to be experts. Learning a new language is not quick or easy, but unlike popular no-mess, no-fuss methods, Optimal Language Learning is actually effective.

Flow is a term coined by the psychologist Mihaly Csikszentmihalyi (1990) that means "the psychology of optimal experience." The opposite of flow is *negentropy,* the equivalent of going nowhere, encountering zero success, slamming into a brick wall. It is negentropy, not flow, that happens too often when many of us attempt to learn a new language.

If you can imagine yourself participating in an activity you love when your mind and body are totally focused on the activity-at-hand, and the task is so challenging that it requires your total concentration and maximum effort to succeed, then you are imagining yourself experiencing flow (Azizi & Ghonsooly, 2015).

People can achieve flow through a variety of experiences—mountain climbing, solving complex scientific problems, running a marathon, writing a story, performing surgery, playing a musical instrument, and—learning to speak a language. The concept of flow has been effectively applied in professional sports, in the boardrooms of corporations, in medical schools, in clinics, and in in the military. *Optimal Language Learning* applies the concept of flow to language acquisition.

For language mavens, learning a new language is a flow experience. For those of us seeking to learn a new language, flow is key. If language learning can be turned into a flow experience, then our time and energy will be meaningfully spent.

Chapter 1 briefly discusses learning theory and psycholinguistics in the context of language learning. Chapter 2 explains the importance of high quality experiences and how the theory of flow can inform how language is acquired. Chapters 3–7 highlight the language learning techniques of five language mavens—Andrew, Emma, Rebecca, Genevieve, and Scott—who possess an uncanny knack for languages.

Like most language learners, these individuals began with a vague curiosity about languages, but unlike most language learners, they took their language skills way beyond basic communicative skills into fluency. Chapter 8 analyzes the similarities and differences among the five language mavens and suggests implications for teaching and learning language.

Only 7 percent of American college students take a foreign language. The number of enrollments in language classes at universities in the United States declined by 111,000 between 2009 and 2013 (Friedman, 2015). Traditional approaches to language study have not been overwhelmingly successful, as less than 1 percent of Americans are proficient in a language that they studied during their K–12 years (Saiz & Zoido, 2005).

Had these five language mavens been solely reliant on traditional approaches, they would have never reached the heights that they achieved. Instead, they took matters into their own hands, took control of their learning, and gained fluency. This book explains how they did it.

Chapter One

Learning and Psycholinguistics

Learning occurs when something new is connected to something old. "Something old" refers to the knowledge the learner already possesses. When "something new" connects with something old in a meaningful way, a person's knowledge expands.

Of course, all learning involves disequilibrium, an imbalance between what is already known and what is encountered. Piaget (1959) contended that learning is basically a constant reorganizational process, involving disequilibrium, adaptation, and restoration. If disequilibrium is too great, the individual may become alienated and shut down. Being exposed to "something new" in a meaningful, non-intimidating way may mollify the sense of imbalance and encourage greater persistence.

Knowledge does not exist exclusively in the individual or in what is to be learned, but in the relationship between the two. Knowledge is constructed by the individual, but is mediated by the environment. That is, knowledge is active and socially driven, the result of a constant negotiation between the individual and the outside world. Two individuals who share the "same experience" do not acquire the same knowledge because each brings a distinctive perspective to the moment-at-hand. The dynamic between old and new, between the individual and the environment helps determine whether language is acquired or forgotten.

Psycholinguistics is the study of the cognitive processes that underlie the comprehension and production of language in the context of the environment in which learning takes place (Harley, 2008). Initially, psycholinguistics tended to focus on the cognitive processes involved in children's acquisition and production of a first language and adults' understanding of language (Schmidt, 1992). Chomsky's work in the late 1950s redefined the study of psycholinguistics by asserting that language is an innate capacity that the brain already possesses, but which also develops and transforms over time (Chomsky & Skinner, 1959; Cenoz, Hufeisen, & Jessner, 2003).

Contrastive Analysis Hypothesis (CAH) focused on the nature of language learners' errors and attempted to attribute errors to specific inadequacies and problems. However, the error-focused techniques of CAH proved to be of limited utility in second language acquisition (SLA) (Compton, 2005; Kellerman, 1986; Lightbown & Spada, 2006). *The Good Language Learner* was a group of academic studies that contended that language learners might benefit more from research on successful language learners than from research on language learners who tried but failed (Selinker, 1972).

KNOWLEDGE OF LANGUAGES AS AN ASSET

As language is tied to culture, children's different background cultures and languages were first perceived as impeding success in schools, creating deficiencies. Both Banks (2004) and Ogbu (1992) proposed that the curriculum accommodate and nurture children's differences to help them reach their full potential. By reasserting the importance of cultural difference, there was also a reaffirmation of the value of knowing more than one language (Cenoz, 2005; Williams & Hammarberg, 1998; Lindqvist, 2009).

In a globalized society, it has become almost compulsory to be multilingual. Whether for developing the intellect, increasing the likelihood of employment, delving into culture, or exploring personal growth, knowing more than one language offers myriad benefits (Bono & Stratilaki, 2009; Christoffels, Haan, Steenbergen, Wildenberg, & Colzato, 2015; Muñoz, 2006). Yet, according to Westly (2011), "only 9 percent of adults in the U.S. are fluent in more than one language. In Europe, that figure is closer to 50 percent" (p. 38).

In Luxembourg, the official languages are Luxembourgish, French, and German, but 60 percent of inhabitants also speak English. In many countries of the Middle East, people know Modern Standard Arabic (MSA), a local dialect, and English. In Japan, students take courses in Japanese, English, and a third language beginning in elementary school (Baines & Yasuda, 2015).

The sheer number of bilinguals among the world's population has stimulated psycholinguistic research on second language acquisition. Indeed, research on bilinguals helps provide additional insight into the role, function, and performance of language in the human brain (Schmidt, 1992).

Research from neuroscience suggests that learning one or more languages enhances executive function, which includes the ability to focus, to understand different perspectives, and to make better decisions (Diamond, 2010; Fan, Liberman, Keysar, & Kinzler, 2015; Poarch & van Hell, 2012; Schwartz,

2011). Being multilingual also helps ward off dementia and results in relatively more white and grey matter in the brain (Olsen, Pangelinan, Bogulski, Chakravarty, Luk, Grady, & Bialystok, 2015).

Knowing more than one language facilitates the development of cognitive skills, including "mental flexibility, abstract thinking and working memory" (Westly, 2011, p. 41). In addition, learning a language opens up new perspectives and new possibilities for living in the world (Martin, 2012).

Learning a new language can be a transformative experience (Kantor, 1936; Lado, 1957; Ortega, 2009). Yet many, if not most, language learners fail to gain fluency and fail to develop a love of the language. In fact, most language learners never attain basic communication skills (Gobel & Mori, 2007; Sahinkarakas, 2011). Part of the challenge is that, for language learning to endure, learning must be intense and persistent. How to intensify and routinize learning for optimal language learning is the subject of chapter 3.

Chapter Two

The Quality of the Experience

In the 1980s, a small group of psychologists came together to discuss the future of psychology as a field. At the time, most psychologists were focused upon studying human misery, mental illness, and an endless universe of neuroses. Rather than study only human beings with problems, it was suggested that, if the goals of psychology were to make people happier and more well-adjusted, then it might be useful to study happy and well-adjusted people as well. Eventually, the field of "positive psychology" was launched and the new emphasis has fundamentally changed perspectives on mental health (Seligman, 2002).

At age 21, the psychologist Csikszentmihalyi (1990) interviewed a group of men from Eastern Europe who had spent years in Stalin's gulag. While all the men shared stories of horror and mistreatment, they also pointed to the time spent in prison as some of the richest years of their lives. Csikszentmihalyi resolved to find out how these men could lead fulfilling lives under cruel, inhumane conditions.

"I wanted to find out how optimal states of being occur and what people can do to bring them about" (Csikszentmihalyi, 1990, p. 3). After decades of studying life satisfaction and peak experiences, Csikszentmihalyi (1990) published his findings in book entitled *"Flow: The psychology of optimal experience"*. In terms of life satisfaction, subjective experience is not just an aspect of life, but "it is life itself" (p. 192).

CONSCIOUSNESS

Consciousness is intentionally ordered information. Information is selected by attention and undergoes cognitive processes that translate the stimuli received through the senses. Sometimes, we focus our attention; other times, external events wrest attention from our control. The pieces of information that integrate into consciousness are coded as experiences and these experiences comprise the basic quality of a life.

When information is processed and stored, it creates a structure for new experiences. The new structure as a core for new experiences is akin to Dewey's concept of building new knowledge by activating students' current knowledge. Because learning is connecting "something old" with "something new" (Schiro, 2013), the approach to language heavily depends on current cognitive structures, as well as *personality traits*.

By understanding and controlling consciousness, a person can improve his or her quality of life. Personality traits such as "*extrovert, high-achiever*, or *paranoid* refer to specific patterns people have used to structure their attention" (Csikszentmihalyi, 1990, p. 33). Certain cultures are predisposed to promote specific personality traits because of traditional, social, and personal practices.

Csikszentmihalyi characterizes attention as *psychic energy*, which determines the very structure of human consciousness. The self is part of consciousness and our conceptions of ourselves are based in large part upon the sum of our experiences. When the self applies a structure to a new experience, the self is altered in a negotiation between what is new and what is old. Therefore, "the self directs attention and attention determines the self" (Csikszentmihalyi, 1990, p. 34) in a dialectical relationship that is mediated by experience, whether the experience is intentional or unintentional.

The opposite of psychic energy is psychic entropy. Psychic entropy, including such elements as pain, fear, rage, anxiety, or jealousy, threatens goals on which the self is focused and impairs the effectiveness of the attention dedicated to specific goals. In effect, psychic energy alters the order of the self. When outside information is congruent with goals, psychic energy flows effortlessly. The battle is not against the self, but against disorder. "It is a battle for the self; it is a struggle for establishing control over attention" (Csikszentmihalyi, 1990, p. 40).

GROWTH OF THE SELF

Consciousness grows and becomes more complex through two psychological processes: differentiation and integration. The mind must be able to differentiate itself from an idea and reconcile with the idea in order to assimilate it. Complexity involves, not only differentiation but also integration of autonomous parts that work together. When "thoughts, intentions, feelings, and all the senses are focused on the same goal, experience is in harmony" (Csikszentmihalyi, 1990, p. 41).

Experience determines who we are. However, experiences cannot always be chosen—many experiences are thrust upon us. For example, the men from Eastern Europe interviewed by Csikszentmihalyi did not volunteer for prison—they were forcibly removed from their homes, sentenced to confinement, and subjugated to torture. But, once in prison, they could have responded in any number of ways. They could have become depressed or angry or they could have decided to adapt and tried to find purpose and joy, despite the dire circumstances in which they found themselves.

While a person cannot always selectively choose experiences, the relationship to those experiences are controllable. Pleasure is "a feeling of contentment that one achieves whenever information in consciousness says that expectations set by biological programs or by social conditioning have been met" (Csikszentmihalyi, 1990, p. 45). For example, when a person is extremely hungry, the taste of food can be especially satisfying.

Enjoyment is more enduring than pleasure. According to Csikszentmihalyi, the elements of pleasure vary little between individuals, regardless of their differences. However, the sense of enjoyment varies by the individual. Despite the allure, pleasure is not concomitant to meaning, especially in the context of self-reflection. The difference between pleasure and enjoyment lies in the involvement of psychic energy. While pleasure does not require the exertion of psychic energy, enjoyment does. When one eats a chocolate, one might feel a momentary sense of pleasure. However, when regularly eating a home-cooked meal with family during childhood, one feels enjoyment.

Flow is a state of enjoyment, not pleasure. For flow to be created, eight basic components have to be present:

1. The task should be perceived as challenging, but reachable.
2. Concentration can take place with no insurmountable obstacles.
3. The task has clear goals.
4. Immediate feedback is provided.
5. Deep but effortless involvement is required that temporarily disconnects the individual from worries and frustrations of everyday life.
6. The individual feels a sense of control or mastery over the action.
7. Although the self disappears during the experience, it reappears stronger after the flow experience.
8. One's sense of time is altered. Hours seem like minutes.

Chapter Two

CLEAR GOALS AND FEEDBACK

When undertaking an activity, clear goals and immediate feedback are necessary. Clear goals involve a certain type of order, and immediate feedback keeps the mind attuned to the activity-at-hand. In addition, some type of challenge must be present in order to feel enjoyment. If the goal is to stay alive while sitting on a couch all day, then clear goals have been set, but challenge would be low.

In contrast, if a mountain climber decides to try to scale Mount Everest, one of the most difficult peaks on earth, the challenge is considerable. With each inch that the mountain climber progresses towards the pinnacle, and with the meeting of each new obstacle—the cold, lack of oxygen, threat of avalanche—the climber would be having a flow experience.

Similarly, writing a book can be considered enjoyable when the author answers a question within a specific amount of time, receives immediate feedback as the pages get filled, organizes thoughts, clarifies ideas, and transforms the research from the realm of the academic to a broader audience. As the challenge gets more difficult, requiring greater and greater effort, experience becomes optimal, and the individual and the action become one.

However, goals and feedback are not always clear, especially in an open-ended activity such as learning a language. How do you know that pronunciation is accurate? If you live in a foreign country, a walk in the street can provide a readily accessible model for the "correct" accent. But, if you are living where the language is not spoken, feedback may be neither accessible nor accurate.

Similarly, when can a language learner claim the attainment of proficiency? Some researchers in second language acquisition have attempted to define language proficiency as ease of speech and fluidity (Guillot, 1999; Kormos, 2006; Riggenbach, 2000; Schmidt, 2002; Segalowitz, 2010). However, there seems to be no universal standard for what constitutes a proficient speaker. Although possible to determine when second language learning starts, it is difficult to ascertain when it ends.

Proficiency is subjective, although a consensus on minimal proficiency is possible. For example, the Test of English as a Foreign Language (TOEFL) is a consensus-based assessment of proficiency used by many institutions of higher education in the United States to assess the readiness of international students for college-level work in English.

For activities like language learning, which can yield widely variable results, the individual performing the action must be able to set the goals and find ways to obtain immediate feedback concerning performance (Egbert, 2004). A language learner can set the goals of being intelligible, speaking like a native speaker, or publishing and presenting work in a setting using the target language.

Self-selected goals allow the individual to establish control over the activity, thereby bringing order to consciousness. When the individual exerts psychic energy towards achieving the self-selected goal, the quality of life is enhanced. In the process of reaching the desired result, the individual should be able to,

- identify the challenge,
- reflect on how the challenge was met,
- derive satisfaction from the successful encounter,
- gain more knowledge about meeting similar challenges in the future.

What constitutes effective feedback depends upon the individual. Although activities that provide a state of flow vary, Csikszentmihalyi (1990) suggests that they must bring order to consciousness and that they all strengthen the structure of the self. "Almost any kind of feedback can be enjoyable, provided it is logically related to a goal in which one has invested psychic energy" (p. 57).

THE AUTOTELIC EXPERIENCE

"The key element of an optimal experience is that it is an end in itself" (Csikszentmihalyi, 1990, p. 67). This might provide some insight into why language learners tend to experience the language and culture differently once they become intelligible. *Intelligibility* does not connote grammatical correctness, but basic communication. Once a language learner becomes intelligible, the focus moves from technical formulation of sounds to the actual expression of meaning.

A communication becomes *autotelic* when it "is done not with the expectation of some future benefit, but simply because the doing itself is a reward" (p. 12). Autotelic experiences bring enjoyment because "life is justified in the present, instead of being held hostage to a hypothetical future" (p. 69). However, an autotelic experience can start out as exotelic, one that is done only for benefits that are exterior to the process itself. That is, experiences can become autotelic over time.

Five characteristics are associated with the autotelic experience:

- clarity,
- centering,
- choice,
- commitment,
- challenge.

Clarity is knowing exactly what is expected. *Centering* is living in the present rather than in the past or future. *Choice* is the feeling of having genuine options. *Commitment* is the assertive decision to expend psychic energy towards achieving a particular goal. *Challenge* is the idea that the degree of difficulty is at an appropriate level—neither too high nor too low.

Once individuals begin engaging in autotelic activities, it is not uncommon for them to actively seek out new opportunities. If a person finds gratification in downhill snow skiing, for example, he or she may decide to seek out and find increasingly challenging downhill courses to try. No one forces them to ski; they seek out new challenges because they are motivated to do so. In other words, the experience of downhill skiing has become autotelic.

GAMES

One way to access a state of flow is to alter reality by giving it a game-like dimension. French psychological anthropologist Caillois (1961) proposed four different categories of world games, as follows:

> *Agon* includes games that have competition as their main feature, such as most sports and athletic events; *alea* is the class that includes all games of chance, from dice to bingo; *ilinx*, or vertigo, is the name he gives to activities that alter consciousness by scrambling ordinary perception, such as riding a merry-go-round or skydiving; and *mimicry* is the group of activities in which alternative realities are created, such as dance, theater, and the arts in general. (p. 72)

According to Csikszentmihalyi games provide opportunities to go beyond the limits of ordinary experience. For example, in agonic games, the players on opposite sides must expand their skills to win, which is the root of the concept of competition. In order to win, players use their skills to push themselves ever further. Soccer, basketball, and tennis are examples of agonic games. In aleatory games, players compete against chance or the future. Playing such games may create a state of flow by providing the player with a sense of control over the future.

Playing poker and other games of chance have an aleatory dimension. Altering the perception of reality is the domain of vertigo games, such as bungee jumping, which simulates the experience of falling, though the individual is safely attached to a large elastic cord.

Mimicry is a type of game where the perception of the self is altered instead of the perception of reality. By pretending to be someone else, such as someone more powerful, a certain state of enjoyment can be attained. Young children, especially, are attracted to playing pretend-games, such as acting like a superhero for a day.

Although separate, two or more of these categories can be observed in the same game. For example, when a soccer player prepares to shoot a penalty kick, in addition to the agonic dimension in which two or more players compete against each other, this specific aspect of the game possesses an aleatory dimension as it is about guessing what the other player will do, which requires predicting the future (Bar-Eli & Azar, 2009).

By practicing an activity in a state of flow, the self acquires a certain set of skills and, in turn, seeks ever-higher challenges, which, in turn, will increase skills. Flow is reciprocal and cyclical. However, flow is possible only if skills and challenges are roughly equivalent. Csikszentmihalyi captures the essence of flow by depicting it as a situation in which task/ability=1. A person's ability must be at its outer limits to meet the difficulty of the task.

Overwhelming challenges, where the task is greater than ability, lead to anxiety, which prevents the individual from enjoying the experience. However, if the experience is not sufficiently challenging, where a person's ability is much greater than the task to be performed, the individual may experience boredom instead of flow. Figure 2.1 is a diagram representing the evolution of the self in a flow state, contrasting it with experiences involving feelings of anxiety and boredom.

Challenges and skills, the two most important aspects of the experience, are represented on the two axes of the diagram. Imagine that the letter A represents a student named Adam at four different times—A1, A2, A3, and A4—during which he is attempting to learn how to speak French as a second language.

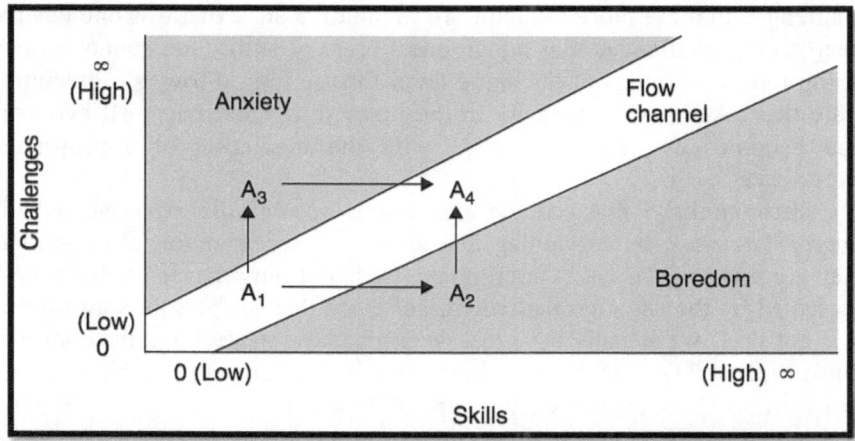

Figure 2.1 Growth of the self in a state of flow (Csikszentmihalyi, 1990, p. 74).

If French were completely new to him, then when Adam started to learn the language during the first few days of class, he might be in state A1. Although his skills were not developed, the teacher spoke mostly in English and the challenges he faced were not difficult. Adam was asked only to memorize one declarative and one interrogative sentence: (1) "*Je m'appelle Adam,*" which is "My name is Adam," and (2) "*Comment t'appelles-tu?*" which is "What is your name?" Adam was enjoying the class because the difficulty of the task matched his rudimentary skills.

From a state of stasis, there are two possible evolutions in experience. In the first case, after a while, Adam might grow tired of repeating the same two phrases again and again, falling into a state of boredom, A2. If the difficulties of future language challenges are not increased, Adam will check out intellectually and find other things to occupy his mind.

In the second case, perhaps Adam's teacher decided to move from the name game to requiring students to read, translate, and recite a long passage from *L'Ecole Des Femmes* by Moliere. Such a difficult assignment for a neophyte language learner would likely throw Adam into a state of anxiety, A3. To bring the task/ability equation back into balance, Adam would have to cram to build his competence enough to complete the assignment.

If Adam succeeds and reads, translates, and recites the long passage from Moliere, he may find himself at A4. Although enjoyable, A4 is not a stable state. Adam will need to encounter even more difficult challenges to match his newly acquired skills or he will fall back into boredom, A2.

Flow is created by sustaining an enjoyable state of growth and discovery. Although the state of A1 is as enjoyable as A4, A4 is different in that it is a more complex experience that demands higher skills to face challenges that are more difficult. To maintain a state of flow, one has to keep facing challenges that match one's level of skill. One cannot enjoy doing the same things at the same level for too long. Flow is a dynamic state that takes place primarily in the inner self. This inner self evolves and becomes ever-more complex with the mediation of appropriate experiences.

Csikszentmihalyi nuanced the expressions *appropriate experiences* and *appropriate skills* by explaining that another factor involving flow is that they are *perceived* as being appropriate. "It is not only the 'real' challenges presented by the situation that count, but those that the person is aware of. It is not skills we actually have that determine how we feel, but the ones we think we have" (p. 75). Flow depends heavily on perception, which means that flow also has subjective and temporal dimensions.

OBSTACLES

When skills increase or challenges increase, the individual can easily slip into a state of anxiety or boredom, which prevents the feeling of flow when performing an activity. Csikszentmihalyi discusses two obstacles that can lead to the development of such states: anomie and alienation.

Anomie is a social condition where the norms of behavior are unclear and disorganized (Durkheim, 1951). Anomie affects individuals who are expected to behave in contradictory ways according to societal expectations. For example, in today's French society, the growing Muslim population is expected to practice their religion in the private sphere, as is promoted by French secularism, but at the same time, they are accused of being too secretive with their religion. In France, the confusion over lifestyles of members of society and the expectations of public decorum have led to anomie.

At the psychological level, anomie occurs when the individual no longer knows what he is supposed to do to take the next step in his evolution. In the context of flow, anomie happens when an individual stagnates and does not know what skills need to be acquired to progress. When learning a language, the feeling of stagnation is comparable to fossilization, the point where an individual plateaus at a certain level of language proficiency.

Alienation is a condition where society's norms are clear, but they stand between the individual and the goal. For example, in some Muslim theocracies, society imposes constraints on the population, especially on women, who do not have equal rights. This creates a condition of alienation for many women. At the psychological level, alienation occurs when the individual knows what the next step is, but cannot take it because of external factors.

When in a state of flow, an individual exposed to a challenge will face obstacles. If he or she does not know what the next step is to continue to be in a state of flow, this will lead to a state of anomie. If, on the contrary, the individual knows what the next step is but cannot take it because of an external constraint, this will lead to a state of alienation. To remain in a state of flow, anomie and alienation must be overcome.

BODY IN FLOW

Flow, experienced primarily in the mind, is a subjective state that is conditioned by the nature of the experience and the nature of our interaction with the experience. The body being the mediator of experience and the mind, it is logical that the body can help determine meaning and interpret the extent to which an experience is enjoyable or unpleasant. Rather than saying that the body experiences flow, it is more accurate to say that the mind experiences flow through the body.

Signals from the body allow the mind to evaluate the data, which assesses the quality of the experience. For example, in language acquisition, out of the four primary skills (writing, reading, speaking, and listening), reading and listening are input-based, and writing and speaking are output-based. Therefore, listening or reading becomes an experience that can inform speaking and writing and the other way around (Sentürk, 2012).

If the experience is repeated in a way that makes it more complex through a system of increasing challenges, immediate feedback, and clear goals, then it will be possible to move into flow. The body then becomes the instrument through which data are evaluated and appreciated.

Because an experience comes to the individual instead of the individual choosing the experience, the individual must be able to analyze what is happening; extract the relevant challenges that match his or her skills; and attempt to bring order to consciousness. For example, a child who is in the school hall waiting for her parents to be done talking to the teacher may find enjoyment in skipping around on the black squares of the checkered floor. She has analyzed the environment, extracted the relevant information of black and white squares, and created a challenge of jumping on black squares only. At a certain point, if her parents take too long, she might lose interest in this activity and increase the speed or the number of squares he can jump on in order to face more difficult challenges. Although this activity is simple, it requires the child to know her body in order to enjoy the experience of taking control over the activity.

The body is the instrument of flow. Performing with the body and understanding the role of the body increases the possibilities for flow. A good language learner usually has an ear for language. A good writer usually enjoys reading. Although there are no clear causal relationships involved with flow, there is a correlation between the sensory perceptions, self-regulatory outcomes, and the development of specific skills.

THOUGHT

Thoughts and experiences are not to be dissociated, but in the flow of thoughts, the primary source of experience is the mind itself. When recalling an experience, the memory of the experience provides enjoyment to the mind instead of the experience itself. Flow can occur in response to memory but also in response to thinking. It is difficult to separate conceptual thinking from memory since "all forms of flow depend on memory, either directly or indirectly" (Csikszentmihalyi, 1990, p. 121).

When Chomsky proposed the concept of Universal Grammar, he raised the question of how the human mind was able to create sentences that it had never previously heard. He suggested that the brain possesses an innate capacity to analyze a sentence, extract the underlying rule (the concept), and apply the rule to a new situation that appears similar to the old one.

For example, when a child says "two tooths," he/she is just using the familiar grammatical rule of adding an S to make a plural. The concept-making device is important because it is the function that helps the mind recognize the experience and apply the appropriate set of skills. When the process of conceptualizing becomes a game with clear goals, immediate feedback, and a match of skills and challenges, the individual can experience flow.

When learning English, some students become fascinated by the language's flexibility. For example, it is possible to turn a proper noun into a verb: "Facebook me," "Google it." Even more surprising, English allows a full sentence to be used as an adjective: "Oh, be careful, she is in her 'I don't wanna talk to anyone' mood." Students can create wild, weird sentences exploiting the language's malleability: "Today, the teacher seems to be wearing his 'I don't wanna appear too serious, but I still need them to read' glasses."

When students are able to play around with language, to make it a game, then language learning can evolve into a flow experience. The important thing is to keep managing the degree of difficulty of the task. Because language proficiency improves with practice, the difficulty of the task must be continually monitored to keep the balance of task/ability=1.

INTRAPERSONAL AND INTERPERSONAL INTELLIGENCE

An autotelic personality promotes a state of flow and improves the quality of experience. The ability to control the experience requires certain knowledge of the self or a sense of intrapersonal intelligence. Gardner's (1983) theory of multiple intelligences values both intrapersonal intelligence (a sense of self) and interpersonal intelligence (a sense of how to interact with others). Csikszentmihalyi explains that the nature of the interactions with others can be a source of enjoyment or pain. "The same person can make the morning wonderful and the evening miserable" (p. 166).

Human qualities, such as generosity, compassion, or empathy, and human defects, such as stinginess, jealousy, or egocentrism, exist only in relationship to others. The qualities and defects of human beings emerge in the context of interactions with others.

Individuals possess an innate need to bond with others. Being alone leads to a feeling of not belonging, of not having a purpose, which can lead to depression. Being alone can stimulate negative experiences, especially if there is nothing that needs to be done.

Finding something worthwhile to do is not easy because "keeping order in the mind from within is very difficult" (Csikszentmihalyi, 1990, p. 169). It is easier for the human mind to find an external activity on which to focus to keep some degree of coherence in our consciousness. When no external activity, such as work, is imposed on us, what people choose to do in their free time is crucially important.

Learning to control consciousness and, by the same token, to control our interaction with experience, is key to self-growth, enjoyment, and improving the quality of life. People who enjoy solitude usually have an ability to structure their consciousness with few external cues. The structure of consciousness is often reflected in the structure of a daily schedule. Being able to enjoy oneself in solitude with a self-imposed discipline, but no external tasks, actually increases the possibilities for flow.

CHEATING CHAOS

Obstacles that present anomie or alienation can hinder flow. Because humans are biological creatures, the mind can take over the body only to a certain extent. However, it should not be assumed that biological impairment automatically translates into anomie or alienation.

Paraplegic participants have reported their accidents to be both the most negative and most positive events of their lives (Massimini, Csikszentmihalyi, & Massimo, 1987). "Cheating chaos" is not a matter of avoiding chaos but facing the challenge and responding to it. The self grows or is destroyed through experience, but there is no such thing as neutrality to experience. An individual can develop coping strategies to accommodate experience, which can be divided in two broad categories: neurotic defense and mature defense.

Neurotic defense is the refusal to deal with problems by avoiding them or by transferring focus onto something else, such as alcohol, video games, or mindless shopping. Mature defense, in contrast, is the ability to temporarily put aside emotions, to analyze problems rationally, and to reassess priorities.

In the mature defense stage, the individual is able to "capture chaos and shape it into a more complex order" (Csikszentmihalyi, 1990, p. 208). He or she transforms adversity into an opportunity for growth. Seen in this context, an obstruction is not the end, but another stage for growth. In that sense, people are not wrong, so to speak; they are just getting closer to the truth. "Few people rely on only one or the other strategy exclusively" (p. 208). Rather, people often go through a neurotic defense stage before entering a mature defense stage.

Csikszentmihalyi suggests three steps in transforming adversity into a compelling challenge:

1. *Unselfconscious self-assurance*: Rather than seeking to dominate the environment, the individual seeks to live in harmony with it.
2. *Focusing attention on the world*: Achieving unity with one's surroundings involves perceiving oneself as part of the environment instead of outside of it.
3. *The discovery of new solutions*: The ability to replace old goals with new ones; the ability to adapt and flourish.

These three qualities are necessary to transform adversity into a meaningful experience. Transforming adversity into an achievable goal is another facet of the autotelic self.

THE MAKING OF MEANING

For life to have meaning, humans need rules for action, a clear focus, and enough psychic energy to devote to worthwhile goals. In other words, the purpose of life is to turn as much of daily life as possible into a series of flow experiences.

Meaning is tightly related to the concept of flow, as it is three-fold. It can be understood in the sense of purpose, as in the question "What is the meaning of life?" Second, it can be understood in the sense of intention, as in the question "What do you mean?" Finally, it can be understood in terms of ordering information, as in the question, "What is worth doing?"

Csikszentmihalyi divided the word *meaning* into purpose, intention, and ordering of priorities (which he calls information). Ideally, the individual will be able to reach harmony in the sense that everything he has done, everything he is doing, and everything he will do fit together into a coherent purpose.

Although it is not possible to reach perfect harmony, the case studies of the language mavens that follow describe moments of flow in diverse ways. Flow is a general concept that can happen at any time to anybody. Like other psychological concepts, measuring flow is not always an exact science that can be determined using precise assessments. However, it is possible to categorize flow into possible causes and expected effects.

Possible Causes of Flow	Expected Effects of Flow
- Setting clear goals	- No sense of time
- Instant feedback	- Accepting the environment "as is"
- Skills match challenges	- Feeling of satisfaction
- Having an autotelic personality	- Doing an activity because you want to (not because you have to)
- Possessing intra/interpersonal intelligence (knowing yourself and/or others)	- Personal growth
	- A sense of control
- Feeling energized	- Self in action

Figure 2.2 Possible causes and expected effects of flow.

Chapter Three

Andrew

"If you want to learn the language, you have to use it over and over in context."

—Andrew Crane

L1=English
L2 (fluent)=Chinese
L2 (some familiarity)=Spanish and Arabic

Andrew teaches in a Center for English as a Second Language (ESL) at a university. He is twenty-eight years old, and he is in his second semester of a master's degree in world-languages education. After an experience as an ESL teacher in China, he is fluent in Chinese and is exploring the possibility of teaching Chinese in K–12 schools in the United States.

His journey to China marked a turning point in his approach to languages and, in a more general way, in his academic and professional life. He grew up in an upper-middle-class family in Tulsa, Oklahoma. He went to a public school, which he described as being "very good and very diverse, although the majority of the kids were white." He has two older sisters, one younger sister, and since his father remarried, Andrew has a half-brother and three stepsisters. His stepmother is Colombian "so half of the family is Hispanic."

Andrew says, "Risk-taking involves not being afraid of change." Most of the people in his home state are scared of change, he says. He is the opposite. He is scared of "non-change." He admits that the members of his family generally live conservatively and avoid taking unnecessary risks, which probably influenced him to be different.

His mother has left her hometown only a few times in her life. He perceives his brothers and sisters as "not really being into languages." From a very early

Figure 3.1 Andrew with a group of some of his students in blue uniforms in Changsha, Hunan, China.

age, he knew he would leave home at some point in his life. All he had to do was to wait for the right opportunity.

INTEREST IN LANGUAGES

Although he does not recall the exact moment he started to be interested in foreign languages, Andrew recalls that video games and animated movies from Japan fascinated him as a child. The "manga culture," as it is called, made him curious about the meanings of the Japanese script that would flitter across the screen.

As he got older, Andrew started reading literature written by Japanese authors, such as Yukio Mishima and Haruki Murakami. Although the readings were in English, his interest in Japanese literature helped stimulate an interest in cultures and languages. As an adolescent, he tried learning Japanese through self-help books and audio, but he gave it up because there were no opportunities to interact with native speakers, no chance to practice.

In seventh grade, Andrew had a social studies teacher, Mr. Smith, who taught geography by connecting it with culture, a connection which made the class lively and interesting. As an undergraduate student at the university, he continued his study of geography, which gave him a genuine sense of the world while it kindled his interest in traveling.

When he got to the university, Andrew decided to enroll in Spanish, "but it did not do anything." In addition to completing the work for class, Andrew tried memorizing long lists of vocabulary words, which led him to increase his lexicon. However, the opportunities to practice Spanish inside and outside of class were scarce. "Learning from the book was not enough," he explains.

He decries the overreliance on English that his university instructor used to teach Spanish. "How many people are actually speaking Spanish? How do you pick up patterns if you don't hear it constantly?" Because of the lack of exposure to the language and the uninspired strategies of his university Spanish instructor, Andrew quickly lost interest.

"They don't teach you in a way where you put together sentences in your mind." Students were not expected to be creative. In fact, experimentation was actively discouraged. Andrew says, "Once you learn the vocabulary list, take the test and move on, you forget."

Despite his disenchantment with Spanish class, Andrew received straight A's. What would have changed his opinion about Spanish would have been "more repetition [of Spanish] in class, more engaging activities, and going to a country like Mexico."

In addition to his underwhelming experience with Spanish, Andrew thought he made poor choices during his time pursuing the bachelor's degree. Because he did not have a precise idea of what he wanted to do, he enrolled in classes that were neither closely related nor countable under a specific degree program.

As a freshman, he was "pre-med," anticipating a future career in the health sciences, but he did not enjoy science courses very much. Then, he took some classes in which he had a genuine interest—sociology and religion. Taking classes in these subjects intensified his interest in cultures, human interactions, and, to a certain extent, languages.

Eventually, Andrew graduated with a bachelor's degree in multidisciplinary studies. He is "not proud of it" because he thinks his degree lacks coherence, and is only a "bunch of credits pasted together."

When discussing learning a language, Andrew compares it to learning to play the guitar. Music "is another type of language," he says. Music is a "combination of sounds that make a meaningful piece." Just as with language, the guitar produces different tones, and it is possible to "play the same thing in ten different ways."

One creates music on the guitar by varying the combinations of chords, rhythms, and speed. By mastering only four chords on the guitar, it is possible to create an endless variety of melodies and songs. When learning a language, once some fundamental "chunks" are learned, it is possible to relay those basic chunks into longer, more complex communications.

Andrew sees his interest in language as part of an ongoing fascination with cultures and traveling. He does not see himself as a "language person" per se, but his life experiences have led him to languages. "It is not like I was born for languages," he said. In fact, when he first set foot in China, he could not speak any other language but English.

MOVING TO CHINA

Upon graduation from college, Andrew decided to look for job opportunities outside his home state. Eventually, he winnowed down the possibilities to two choices. The first job involved working in a vineyard in Oregon. The prospect of living in a beautiful area of the country, interacting with nature, and earning a good salary was very attractive. The second job involved working 9 a.m. to 5 p.m. in a business office.

Although the salary was good, the sedentary nature of the job and the nature of the work were not appealing. Just as he was deciding to move to Oregon, Andrew received an email that, according to him, "looked like a fraud." Its subject line was, "Go to China and teach!"

Although the email seemed like just another piece of spam, Andrew decided to investigate. One of the things he learned during his investigation was that, to move to China, he needed to get a work visa.

As he was gathering information on the work visa, he learned that the opportunity to teach in China was "not a scam," but a legitimate possibility for employment. He applied, got the job, and obtained the visa. His initial plan was to stay for a year. "I saw an opportunity to go abroad, and I just took it. I was ready." Deciding to go to China was an "impulsive decision." In Andrew's view, his spontaneity is both an asset and liability.

Before going to China, Andrew did not set goals for himself, or at least, he did not have goals pertaining to learning the Chinese language. His basic plan was to travel to a foreign country, teach English, and then travel around from there as much as possible. While Andrew acknowledged the need to understand Chinese to be functional in his everyday life, he believed that English was going to be "enough to get around." He admits that, "I did not know what I was doing."

Andrew explains that it is beneficial to have a mentor or friend proficient in the language who can answer questions that inevitably arise. When he first arrived at the Shanghai airport, he was lucky enough to become friends with a fellow teacher who had been in China for four years and knew the language well. They exchanged contact information.

Since they lived close to each other, they would talk daily, usually about aspects of the language and local customs. This unplanned mentor relationship helped Andrew a great deal. "It is not like I wanted to be as good as him," he said, but seeing an American speak Chinese so well made him realize that gaining mastery over Chinese was not an insurmountable undertaking.

FUNCTIONAL CHINESE

An old, Chinese man on a train once advised Andrew that, when learning a new language, "Your facial skin needs to be thicker than the Great Wall." Having thick skin and being fearless are traits that were common among the people Andrew encountered in China who had successfully learned the language. He notes that other traits that seemed to help were being extroverted and having a natural curiosity.

Once he arrived in China, Andrew decided to learn the language by studying topics that were related to "realistic situations such as going to the bank, buying train tickets, or buying food at the supermarket." He reasoned that, if he studied a host of practical phrases, then he would have more opportunities to speak to people while conducting his daily activities.

To refresh his memory when walking around in public, he would always carry a notebook and write down new words as he encountered them. The notebook was also used to record notes to himself, to jot down general observations, or to record phrases overheard in conversations.

After learning new vocabulary terms and grammatical rules, he would write sentences using those new words and rules as he felt an urgent need to "apply the language" right away, to make it stick. He realized that, if he learned vocabulary words but did not practice them in this manner, they would be lost—like he lost the meanings of the Spanish words that he had furiously memorized as an undergraduate in college.

In the early stages of learning Chinese, Andrew found it necessary to practice writing new vocabulary words at least an hour per day to make him feel like he was making progress with the language. In his experience, it typically took three days of practice before he could remember a new word well enough to use it without referring to his notes.

He stresses the importance of repetition when learning from a book or through oral communication. "If you say a word once, you will inevitably forget the word. If you say a word a thousand times, you will remember it for many years."

As a neophyte to China, Andrew also tried to learn as many cultural aspects of the language as possible. "In Chinese, it is customary to learn about the regional differences in cuisine, the customs of the 56 minority groups, the major festivals, and famous works of literature." He made a conscious effort to make cultural references to food while dining at local restaurants, to recite poems during meetings or class talks, and to get into discussions with Chinese of a particular region about their local culture. When he was mingling with Chinese in daily life, he felt a little strange in that he always seemed to be "performing," rather than simply "being" part of the community.

After a few months, Andrew learned a few key phrases in Chinese. He had memorized phrases such as "nǐhǎo," (你好, "hello") or "duōshǎo qián" (多少钱, "how much money"), and he was more or less understood on the street. However, he still had a hard time understanding some native speakers. For example, when he got into a taxi with his American friend who was

Figure 3.2 Andrew discusses Spring Festival paper cuts with an artist in Shigu Ancient Town, Yunnan, China.

fluent in Chinese, the friend would do all the interacting with the taxi driver while Andrew would fall silent. Andrew knew that the journey from knowing selected chunks of the language to gaining mastery would require a significant amount of effort, but that night in the taxi, he decided that he would become proficient in Chinese.

Coincidentally, shortly after this decision, the apartment where he was living had an extended power outage. As a result, there was "no light, no access to the Internet, no TV, nothing." Because he had nothing to distract him, Andrew decided the time was right to begin studying Chinese intensively.

Rather than play around on the Internet or watch TV, he started spending long hours, sometimes as many as eight hours a day, studying. He would study before work, walk over to the school to teach (the school was conveniently located next to his apartment), return home, and begin studying again.

The notebook with which he was taking occasional notes became his constant companion. He would systematically draw and memorize "about 40 characters in three days." He would write characters in his notebook ten times, and then flip the page and rewrite them from memory.

After memorizing a character and its corresponding tone(s), he began an extended study of grammar. He would combine newly learned words with a new grammatical rule. He would go outside after studying and practice with locals the sentences or words he had just memorized. He would ask them questions such as, "Where is the library?" to start a conversation and then proceed from there as an excuse to keep the exchange going.

The content he was using did not vary much because he memorized sentences in chunks. "I would say the same things over and over." Although many of his "trial conversations" with locals were successful, he would still practice words and phrases repeatedly so as not to forget what he had just learned. Although it was "tedious work," Andrew considered this intense repetition as absolutely necessary for his continued growth.

LANGUAGE EPIPHANY

One day, when practicing his sentences with a clerk in a grocery store, Andrew suddenly realized that he was finally able to have a normal conversation with a native speaker. He explained that, "it is not like from one day to another; I understood everything," but the move to competence was startling nevertheless.

It gave him the confidence to start experimenting with the language and to try out new ideas. He would combine several sentences together, try out new words, ask questions, and actively negotiate meaning.

"Suddenly, things started to click. That's the best way to describe it ... It all hits you all at once. You can put together all these words in your speech, and everything speeds up."

One interesting breakthrough was understanding not only his areas of strength, but also where he was falling short. Being functional in the streets reinforced his decision to study on a regular basis. When the electricity in his apartment was fixed a week later, he decided to forego his usual entertainments so that he could continue his focus on learning Chinese.

Although Andrew was not fluent in Chinese at this point, he characterized this short, concentrated bout of studying during the power outage to be the turning point in the evolution of his language proficiency. In describing his epiphany, Andrew stressed two aspects of the experience as key:

1. His willingness to be creative as soon as things started to "click."
2. His consciousness about the exact moment that he became conversational in Chinese and the abruptness of the epiphany.

Andrew explains that, if he possessed the skills before the epiphany, he did not exploit them, so, in effect, they did not exist. His competence with Chinese "popped up really fast" and, as his results improved, he became ever more driven to master the language.

When signing up to go to China, Andrew's original plan was to work for a year and then return home. At the end of his first year, he reflected that, for much of his time in China, he had been in survival mode, just trying to get by. He had overcome a series of challenges, including becoming conversant in a difficult language, pretty much on his own, and he had successfully worked as a teacher of English in a local school.

Although Andrew did not know how much longer he might stay, he wanted to extend his Asian adventure. In China, there was "always something to do," at least compared to his hometown, and his experiences, by and large, had been pleasant. Secondly, he was starting to enjoy teaching, which was "a whole new experience that was challenging and fun." Finally, he was getting better at the Chinese language, and he wanted to see how far his learning might take him.

The challenge of the language was tied up with the novelty of living in a foreign culture. Andrew ended up staying in China for two more years, and during those two years, he made a transition in his study routine, moving from a reliance on books and notes to a focus on interactions with locals.

Although he still used books, they became secondary to primal experience. Rather than experiencing a "second epiphany," he felt that the additional expertise he acquired over the next two years was layered atop the foundation of his "first epiphany," which was created out of the desire to speak well, aided by intensive study, and instigated after an extended loss of power at his apartment.

PHOTOGRAPHY

Andrew liked the city where he worked because it was diverse, and he spent a lot of time socializing with people who were French, British, and American, as well as Chinese. Some of his newfound friends were journalists, and they influenced his perceptions of the culture and the society. They also encouraged him to record his experiences through photographs and written descriptions. "I got really good at photography," he says.

As with music and language, Andrew also sees parallels between photography and language. For example, he notes that no two people see buildings, flowers, or sunsets in exactly the same way. He tells the story that, one day, he walked by a beautiful garden of flowers and decided to take a picture.

He had an image in his mind of the kind of photograph that he wanted to take, so he found a ladder, climbed to the top rung, and took the picture that "he had in mind." His perspective of the flower from atop the ladder would be quite different from a photographer standing on the ground. Andrew notes (with nonchalant profundity) that differences in perspective determine differences in outcome.

Andrew contends that photography requires being active, rather than passive. Instead of waiting for the right shot, the right angle, or the right moment, a good photographer creates it. When learning Chinese, Andrew explains, it was essential to be creating the "right moments" by going outside and talking to people rather than waiting for the "right moments" to come so that "you can use a newly learned word." Exposure is not enough. A language learner must be active, not passive.

Both photography and language learning rely upon repetition. Learning certain language skills requires sustained repetition. Repetition is tolerable and beneficial as long as it culminates in a meaningful experience or an opportunity to apply what has been learned. A photographer may take the same kind of photo repeatedly, but at some point, there has to be a purpose—a photo framed and displayed at home or entered into a contest.

For repetition to be effective, there must be an evolution from replication to application. Once repetition is able to engender an appropriate, automatic response, a creative response becomes possible. It is with the engagement of the creative mind that learning takes off.

Chapter Three

THE RETURN

In his third and final year in China, Andrew became a kind of local celebrity. He was in high demand as a speaker to large assemblies of students at universities and to auditoriums full of teachers and K–12 students. He was interviewed on the radio and was featured on TV. Andrew wound up teaching English for several schools and agencies. One of the last agencies for which he worked promised him a big paycheck, but never delivered it. He filed a complaint with the agency and the local police department. At first, his complaints were not taken seriously, but eventually he received reprimands and threats of bodily harm that seemed quite serious. So, Andrew felt that he had no choice but to flee the country.

In addition to teaching two Chinese courses at a high school and teaching English at a Center for ESL at the university, today Andrew is "playing around" with Arabic and thinks he might want to explore teaching English as a foreign language in the Middle East in the near future.

He confesses that he likely will not be able to master Arabic while living in the United States because there are too few Arabic speakers. "Language needs to be immediately applicable," he says, used "consistently in a real context." When immersed in a language and culture, learning is "not studying but fun." Unless he decides to move to a country where Arabic is the dominant language, Andrew predicts that he will lose both his vocabulary and his desire to learn Arabic.

As an instructor of Chinese in the United States and an instructor of English for non-native speakers, Andrew relies upon what he learned from his struggles to learn the rudiments of Chinese. Because he found success in learning "chunks" of language, he introduces words in meaningful combinations. For example, he teaches a verb with an object, first separately, then together. His goal is to have his students "automatize" certain foundational chunks in the target language so that they can move on to creative uses of the language and eventually, learn to construct sentences of their own.

As he emphasizes the practicality of language, he concentrates on high-frequency words, especially in the beginning, to build a knowledge base. For one lesson, for example, he teaches vocabulary suitable for a restaurant because the most likely place for his American students to speak Chinese, apart from hanging out with a group of Chinese students, is in a Chinese restaurant.

Although not ideal, speaking Chinese at a Chinese restaurant would at least give students the opportunity to use the language in authentic ways. However, he notes that most students are reticent to speak because they do not want to embarrass themselves by making mistakes. To learn a language, Andrew implores, a student must do "his or her part of the job," step out of the bubble, and enter the real world.

Figure 3.3 Andrew at the helm of an ox-driven rickshaw during a Rapeseed Flower Festival in Luoping, Yunnan, China.

ANALYSIS

Andrew's approach to language learning started out haphazardly but became increasingly systematic over time. When he was first exposed to foreign languages, he did not have the metalinguistic skills to become an autonomous learner. With his experience in China, he had to develop sophisticated language skills just to survive.

He would acquire vocabulary, memorize certain sentences, and replicate these words and phrases in real contexts to create an experience with the word. As for grammar, he believes that patterns can be acquired with regular exposure to the language, which is called *implicit grammar instruction* in the field of second language acquisition (SLA), as opposed to *explicit instruction*, which relies on teaching the rule first.

Andrew's Spanish classes at the university tended towards explicit instruction, offered few interactive experiences, and did not allow him (or other students) to control any aspect of their own learning. Although he was a good student who could recite endless lists of Spanish vocabulary on demand, Andrew quickly became bored because the content and the degree of difficulty never changed. The number of words he knew increased, but the challenge was static, centered on committing words and phrases to memory. While Andrew learned grammatical rules and a few phrases in Spanish, most instruction was in English, making the class artificial and "mind-numbing."

The accumulation of Spanish vocabulary meant little without application. His Spanish instruction was input-based. He received information, but was required to produce little in response. Freire would say that, in the case of his Spanish class, Andrew was the object rather than the subject of his education. If the class had been taught in Spanish, if students had been required to create sentences of their own, if a shift would have been made to practical usage, Andrew might have developed "an ear for the language" as well as a love for it.

Obviously, Andrew never experienced flow in his Spanish class, and as a result, he did not look for opportunities to practice the language outside of class. His disgust over the non-engaging style of the instructor carried over to a general disinterest in Spanish language and culture. Andrew did not consider learning Spanish an enjoyable activity, so he saw no reason to pursue it, though his stepmother, and half-brothers and sisters were from Columbia and were fluent speakers of Spanish.

An advantage of plopping down in a country where you do not speak the language is that you receive regular instant feedback when you interact with locals and you are able to monitor your proficiency daily. In Andrew's case, he started his study of Chinese by identifying specific interactions of daily life, such as "buying food at the supermarket." According to Csikszentmihalyi (1990), Andrew was *preparing the kind of interaction* he was going to have. As his skills evolved, he created ever-higher goals.

The initial goal was to be functional and understood by local Chinese, so Andrew acquired and tried to master "chunks" of vocabulary and grammar. The next step was to move into being creative with the language. To assess his relative success, he used the abundant and immediate feedback of the people on the street with whom he interacted every day.

Andrew's ability to gain some degree of control over his experience is highly correlated with the confidence needed to "play around" with the language. Being creative with the language means actively manipulating it. Language researcher Swain (2005) argues that language use has a prominent role in learning a L2 because interactions involve both receiving input and producing output.

Routinization and practice lead to automaticity, which makes the cognitive load of moving to fluency much easier. Initially, through intensive study and continual self-monitoring, Andrew was able to develop his own stepping stones to learning the language. From his practice of rehearsed sentences, Andrew moved to a regimen of daily, prolonged interactions with native speakers, which allowed him to keep moving the bar higher and higher. He went from being able to greet people and introduce himself to being able to take a taxi and buy items in a supermarket to moving almost effortlessly through daily life.

Although linguists might attribute Andrew's success with Chinese as testimony of the veracity of socio-cultural theory (SCT) or the "output hypothesis," his experience can also be viewed in terms of flow. Flow theory does not contradict SLA theories; rather, flow theory helps explain language acquisition at the individual level.

While the output hypothesis and SCT are theories that take place in the objective world, flow is a subjective state that depends on the learner's perception of his or her emotions and the intensity of engagement while performing a particular task. Flow explains how a language learner can gain skills that enable mastery far beyond what they might have imagined.

In Andrew's case, learning a language was situated within the broader context of learning how to live in a completely new environment. Andrew needed to be functional in the target language if he wanted to survive. However, he needed other skills as well, such as being sociable, learning correct etiquette, and navigating his job as teacher within the context of being a single young man in a foreign land.

At the end of his first year, Andrew started to exert some control over the Chinese language. Possessing new skills and enjoying the feeling of having acquired them, he decided to increase the challenge by staying in China for two more years. In a way, language became just one part of larger skill set that involved integrating into Chinese society as a full-fledged member, at least to the extent that a white foreigner could become a full-fledged member of Chinese society.

Andrew managed to adapt to his environment, identified the necessary skills he would need, then set out to acquire them. Once he acquired a certain skill, he would use the newly acquired skill to go after more complex skills.

Over time, a connection emerged between his love of language and his love for photography that went beyond an interest in culture. As he began to blossom as a speaker of Chinese, he also began to grow as an artist and a photographer.

Recently, Andrew published a book for students beginning their study of Chinese called *Practical Chinese: Beginner Level I.* The book distills for language learners the kind of preparation that he wished he had had before coming to live in China.

Andrew's photographs have quickly gained a large Internet following, and he has won a few awards, including one from *National Geographic* magazine. A collection of his photography can be found at https://andrewjcrane.wordpress.com/.

Chapter Four

Emmanuelle

"Learning languages is learning about people."

—Emmanuelle Chiocca

L1=French
L2 (fluent)=English, Spanish, Chinese
L2 (some familiarity)=Latin, Greek, Hebrew, Hungarian, Lakota, Cherokee, Italian

Emmanuelle (Emma) is twenty-seven years old. She is a French student enrolled in a doctoral program focusing on world-languages education at a university in the southwest. She never thought, until recently, that she would ever be a teacher. Although she became interested in languages very early in her life, the desire to become a language teacher has only recently emerged.

Emma was born in France and half of her family is from Spain. She learned her second language, Spanish, from a great aunt and uncle at the same time she was learning her native language, French. By definition, Emma is a simultaneous bilingual speaker. It was not that her great aunt and uncle did not know a lot of French; they simply preferred Spanish, as Spanish was their first language.

Growing up, Emma heard French everywhere outside, but when she was with her grandparents or around her great uncle and aunt, the spoken language was Spanish. After Emma's great aunt (the matriarch) died, the prevalence of Spanish in the household waned, and the official language at home evolved from Spanish to French.

From this childhood experience, Emma developed empathy for immigrants and "outsiders." Emma's grandmother, sister, and great aunt and uncle had

34   *Chapter Four*

Figure 4.1 Emmanuelle plays around in a castle in the south of France. Emma's disposition towards languages was quite playful.

fled Spain at different points in time. With the stories of her grandparents and the emphasis they put on speaking Spanish, Emma realized as a little girl that language was intermingled with culture. At age three, she entered the French public school system.

LANGUAGES IN SCHOOL

When she entered the educational system in France, foreign languages were not part of the curriculum in elementary school. In middle school, however, choosing a second language was compulsory. When she turned eleven, she started to learn English and she immediately liked it, though she also liked other subjects.

At heart, she was "just a schoolgirl" who liked going to school. She recalls being very studious, motivated, and excited at school. She liked language classes, especially, and put a lot of effort into them because she "liked to have good grades" and enjoyed receiving validation from her teachers, parents, and peers.

She explains that her junior high English-language courses were grammar-based and mostly meaning-free. She cannot recall "a single instance of cooperative learning, such as turn-to-your-partner, team building activity, jigsaw, think pair share, concept cards, brainstorming, or any use of multi-sensory prompts." Instead, class mainly consisted of group recitations with individual recitations on occasion. The interactions were always between teacher and student, never student to student. English was taught via a regimen of repetition, supplemented by Total Physical Response (TPR) exercises, which she hated.

TPR is a language-teaching philosophy that coordinates teacher's commands using the target language with student's physical movements. For example, a teacher might say, "Touch the tip of your nose!" The indication of comprehension would be the number of students interpreting the command correctly by touching their nose. The idea is to connect foreign words and phrases with real phenomenon so that the student can associate new words with familiar objects.

One reason Emma hated TPR was because it did not seem to work very well. She and her peers rarely responded to teacher commands at all, and when they did, they often responded incorrectly. Emma's early English education "could have been better." She believes that "pedagogy and creativity were not part of the education these teachers had received."

The only cultural artifact in her junior high English class was a flag of the United Kingdom, though the teacher rarely (if ever) spoke about life or culture in the United Kingdom during class. In France, English education is linguistically and culturally influenced by the United Kingdom, especially England.

However, her dad always had been interested in Native American cultures and her grandmother had been impressed with American soldiers in Paris at the end of World War II (WWII), so the cultural reference point for the English language for Emma was the United States, not England.

LATIN AT TWELVE

At age twelve, Emma started to learn Latin because she was very interested in mythology, and "because my dad forced me." Her father had always put a strong emphasis on knowing the French language and speaking it well, and he thought that Latin would contribute positively to her mastery of French. According to some members in her family, especially on the Spanish side, proficiency in French was not only essential for proper integration into French society, but would be important for academic purposes, as well.

Her teachers of Latin focused on grammar, repetition of cases, and long lists of vocabulary. The basic pattern for Latin class was to commit long lists of words to memorization, then to apply memorized concepts to exercises on worksheets. Although she felt like Latin was of negligible value when she was an adolescent, now she feels that Latin has given her insight into the logic of language, aided her understanding of grammatical structures, and allowed her to guess the meanings of unfamiliar words in a variety of different languages. Latin also helped her understand concepts better in subjects as diverse as philosophy, biology, and physics.

Once, when working on her master's thesis in history, she needed to use a work that meant, "taking effect from a date in the past." She did not think such a word existed in the English language, so she used her knowledge of French and Latin to create what she thought was a made-up word, based upon the French *retroactif*, and Latin *retroact*, past participle stem of *retroagere*. Only later did she come to realize that she did not create a new word—*retroactive* was already a widely accepted word in the English language. In this way, she thought that Latin allowed her to be creative with language.

SPANISH AT THIRTEEN

At the age of thirteen, it was compulsory to choose a second foreign language in middle school. Depending on the school, there might be two, three, or more languages to choose from, the most popular being Spanish, German, and Italian. Emma chose Spanish, mainly because of her family heritage. She wanted to know more about the culture, the people, and the country her relatives had fled.

Like all her school subjects, Emma loved Spanish. However, Spanish was taught the same way that English had been taught, "with lists of vocabulary and expressions no real thirteen-year-old Spanish girl would ever say, old documents, old expressions, old pictures, old texts, old movies." She explained that her motivation was intrinsic, which is why the dull presentation of the subject did not turn her off completely.

She continued her study of Spanish into high school and, as she improved her knowledge of the language, she grew more interested in Spanish culture. She enjoyed studying Spanish "for the culture and not for the grades." Through the Spanish language, she reconnected with her roots and revived the dormant tongue of her early childhood. She calls her first Spanish experience "an aborted bilingualism," in that it was a period of immersion (in conversations "inside the house") that lasted until age six, then disappeared completely. She emphasizes that her interest and motivation for relearning Spanish grew from an interest in family heritage.

ANCIENT GREEK AT FIFTEEN

At the age of fifteen, Emma started learning Ancient Greek because she was fascinated by Greek history and mythology, and "because, again, father had decided." She started studying Ancient Greek while she was still studying Latin, English, and Spanish. She quickly realized how useful both Latin and Greek were to help her expand her vocabulary.

On the surface, Greek was similar to Latin, in that the language would not help her start up conversations with anyone currently living on the planet. Also, like Latin, the insights offered by the language was into a culture that ceased to exist thousands of years ago. As with her previous language classes, Ancient Greek mostly involved memorization.

However, for one period every week, her Greek teacher would teach a "civilization hour," in which the emphasis was on how Ancient Greek civilization contributed to modern-day Europe. The teacher used a words-in-context approach, and used moments in history as a means to introduce new vocabulary. Although Emma did not learn etymologies or key dates any better than grammar rules, she often connected what she learned in "civilization hour" to her other courses, particularly in the social studies. Emma liked thinking that all learning, regardless of subject matter, was interconnected.

ENGLISH AND HEBREW AT SIXTEEN TO SEVENTEEN

At the age of sixteen, Emma decided to work on English outside of school, mainly because she was fond of American pop-culture. At the same time, she became fascinated by Hebrew and began exploring the language in a local Jewish cultural center. She had been introduced to the history of Israel in conversations with her dad and in history class and, in fact, the Jewish Diaspora "was all around her." As part of his job, her father traveled several times to Israel and the Second Intifada with the Palestinian people was "everywhere on the news."

At age seventeen, Emma participated in a language program and spent a month in California, allowing her to finally become completely immersed in American culture. Immersion in an English-speaking culture was exactly "what I wanted" in that she had to use her English every day without fail. She liked the feeling of being able to communicate with people she did not know who were "from so far away." The following summer, she participated in a second student exchange program, this time in Pennsylvania.

LEARNING LANGUAGE IN SECONDARY SCHOOL

Emma earned excellent grades in language classes because she found foreign words, phrases, and culture, fascinating. Although her language classes were uniformly uninspiring, they seemed more vital to her than other classes. Even the walls of her most mundane language classes were decorated with at least a few artifacts from a different place, and other locations around the world seemed incomprehensible and mysterious.

Another attractive attribute of language classes is that they were more "laid back" than other classes. Whereas the curricula of "core classes" such as mathematics, science, and history seemed fixed and immutable, the content of language classes was flexible and contingent. What Emma appreciated particularly about language classes is that there was not always one right answer, but several right answers.

Although she sometimes had a tepid response to the intricacies of grammatical labels and spelling rules, she leapt at the opportunity to express an opinion or to figure out how to creatively phrase a question. Such moments in her classes seemed like when real learning was occurring, not when she was asked to "mechanically apply something previously acquired."

The first task in all of her language classes was to introduce herself in the Target Language; no other classes encouraged personal introductions. Furthermore, the goal of language classes was usually on the development on the self, on how the self could adapt to a new way of looking at the world through the lens of a new language. With language, there was no disguising ineptitude, just as there was no hiding proficiency. Students could either communicate competently or they couldn't. In other subjects, proficiency was less necessary and less obvious. In core classes at school, the content was king; the self was almost superfluous. Core classes explained the world; language classes enabled a student to actively participate in it.

One of the most glaring omissions from her secondary schooling was the lack of attention to interdisciplinary connections. The French educational system follows a national curriculum, which dictates the precise number of subjects and levels that each student must take. As a result, content areas tend to become independent silos and there may be little communication among teachers of different subjects or at different levels at a school.

Emma elaborates, "In theory, they're supposed to look for interdisciplinarity, but in practice, each subject is locked within itself." To try to "connect the dots," Emma gradually started to search for material outside of the classroom and outside of the school. For example, she bought and read books written in English and watched English-language movies on a daily basis. She read the original version of *Harry Potter* and watched the movie with English subtitles "about a hundred times." As she read books and watched movies, she always brought along her trusty notebook so that she could jot down new words and phrases as she encountered them.

When watching the movie *Gladiator*, she heard the expression "busy like a bee," scribbled it in her notebook and made a mental note to use the phrase at the next opportunity. She was aware that she would not learn idioms, slang, or any "cool stuff" in the classroom because classroom instruction tended towards the formal, simplistic, and mechanical.

Emma listened and tried to understand the lyrics of popular American and British bands; she played video games in English; she perused English-language websites. She perceived these "outside of school" activities as essential for honing her knowledge of vocabulary, grammar, and pronunciation. Although it could be "a lot of homework," raiding popular culture was also "a lot of fun" and is a major reason that her fascination with English endured.

Her dalliances with popular culture made her feel empowered and a little subversive in the sense that she was using unsanctioned material that had not received the blessing of her teachers. Emma estimates that she spent more time watching movies, listening to music, and reading in English than doing class work and that she learned far more about the language outside of class than in class.

HUNGARIAN

As an undergraduate at a university in the southwest of France, Emma took a class in Hungarian, "but this time, not by passion but because I was required to take a semester of a non-Indo-European language." Her initial choice was Arabic. However, since Arabic classes were already full, she decided to go with the only other choice, Hungarian.

Her Hungarian teacher taught using complete immersion. No language but Hungarian was allowed during class. Emma claims that the teacher never addressed her, even in casual encounters in the hallway, in any language other than Hungarian. While the immersion experience was stimulating, it also stressed her out and made her continually nervous. Her teacher would work off of real materials, such as newspapers and magazines in Hungarian, but in spite of the teacher's best efforts, she did not feel any connection to the language or the culture.

She was taking Hungarian as a requirement and decided to have fun with it, but she wanted to do just enough to pass the class and nothing more. Perhaps one reason for her disinterest was, unlike English, Emma had no particular interest in Hungary or its culture. Second, she did not have a positive rapport with her teacher. Her rapport was not negative; she just did not have much of a relationship with him.

Emma confessed to remembering little from her Hungarian class other than a few greetings and some stock phrases. She remembered more from her Latin and Hebrew classes taken years earlier. Without an active interest in the language or culture, Emma transformed into a more "typical" or "average" student in her language acquisition.

MORE ENGLISH, LAKOTA, AND ITALIAN IN COLLEGE

Emma maintained an interest in English and in American culture, so she decided to pursue a Bachelor of Arts in English with a specialization in teaching French as a Second/Foreign Language in France. She graduated when she turned twenty-one and, after graduation, she spent a month in England. The month in England was a transformative experience that "did something" to her.

Before England, she was an extremely shy, awkward, and introverted girl. After England, she became an outgoing, graceful, ebullient young adult. When her parents visited her in England, they did not speak English, so they relied on her to translate, which she did with aplomb. Her expertise with English made a lasting impression on her parents. "The fact that my parents kinda needed me for the first time affected my personality in a good way and made me feel empowered."

Because she had always been interested in Native American cultures, in general, and in Lakota history, in particular, Emma started trying to learn the Lakota language on her own, just a few words for fun—numbers, animals, and family. Eventually, she applied as an exchange student to the University of Oklahoma's history program in 2009 where she would be able to take classes in Native American History and Native American Literature.

While many students initially decide to go on an exchange program abroad to learn the language, Emma's primary motivation was to meet the people of Oklahoma and learn about Native American cultures. She was confident that her English skills were good, although she still wanted to improve. At this point in her life, Emma had started to think in English. Like Andrew, she remembered the exact moment when English transformed from being a cognitive ordeal to an ordinary, reflexive response. "One day, when I was living in London, I suddenly realized that I was not thinking in French anymore. I was thinking and speaking in English."

At University of Oklahoma, Emma took three classes, all of which pertained to Native Americans: Native American History, Native American

Literature, and Native American Studies. Emma says that the process of connecting thoughts on Native American culture was like making a quilt. When you are sewing each piece, you are focused only on a small patch of fabric. Then, you have a kind of a *"gestalt,"* as Emma put it, and a picture of the entire quilt emerges. "Everything becomes greater than the sum of its parts."

During summer 2009, Emma traveled to Italy for vacation, so she taught herself Italian before she left. She used her previous knowledge of French, Spanish, and Latin, "as bridges" to Italian, which made learning the language "relatively easy." However, Emma insists that her knowledge of Italian is only on "a tourist level."

FRENCH IN AMERICA

Emma reasoned that being a native speaker of French in a graduate program in the French Department at a university would make it easier to get a job as an instructor. As a teaching assistant, Emma learned that she would get her tuition waived and receive a small stipend. The pay was substantially less than spectacular, but such an arrangement would allow her to gain more experience in an English-speaking environment, give her a way to continue her study of Native American cultures, and make pursuing an advanced degree financially feasible.

Teaching French in the United States was a "revelation." "There is nothing quite like teaching your own culture, your own references, and your own language." Remembering the stale instruction and minimalist approach to languages from her secondary schooling, Emma pledged to herself that she would imbue French culture in every class that she taught. In fact, Emma viewed the French language a vehicle for understanding French culture. A culture-centric approach seemed only natural, as she thought that there was no legitimate way to separate language from culture.

In Emma's French classes, she strived to use meaningful activities and authentic materials. Her parents would send her magazines and newspapers on a regular basis as well as food and candies. She organized a "candy week" and had students sample a different type of candy every class period. She also used pictures, cartoons, songs, music videos, maps, and timelines to help students better understand the French culture and language.

"I really bonded with my students, and met several of them in France last summer and this summer, while they were studying or traveling in France." Rather than only take the minimal classes as required by their degree programs, many of Emma's students went deeper into the language, eventually changing their majors or minors to French.

Figure 4.2 Emmanuelle hikes in Palo Duro Canyon in the Texas Panhandle. Emma's interest in Native American culture, history, and literature also spurred her interest in Native American languages.

Emma's overwhelmingly positive student evaluations earned her an award, given by the provost of the university to instructors who were highly ranked by their students. Only instructors whose rank was in the top 10 percent of all instructors were eligible for the award.

To her great surprise, teaching French at the university became one of the most meaningful experiences of Emma's life. Although she had taught other subjects in different settings, teaching her native language to non-native speakers had given her a visceral thrill. After one year of teaching French, she accepted a position at the Center for English as a Second Language (CESL) so that she could teach English to non-native speakers. (CESL is the same kind of center where Andrew, featured in the previous chapter, was employed.)

Emma accepted the position at CESL because the curriculum was flexible and different from previous teaching experiences.

TEACHING NON-AMERICAN, NON-ENGLISH-SPEAKING STUDENTS

CESL prepares international students from non-English-speaking countries to pass the TOEFL (Test of English as a Foreign Language) so that they can apply to universities in English-speaking countries. Without a passing score on the TOEFL, international students cannot get accepted into colleges or universities in the United States or abroad.

In January 2014, Emma started the job at CESL and immediately encountered a large number of Chinese students. A friend told her that the Confucius Institute was offering free Mandarin classes on campus. As soon as she heard about the free classes, Emma began organizing her schedule to accommodate all of her goals and interests. She decided to learn Chinese at the Confucius Institute twice per week in the afternoons, to maintain her teaching schedule at CESL, and to take graduate classes in the evenings.

Of course, Chinese students at CESL knew that Emma was a French graduate student teaching English, one who was also simultaneously trying to learn Chinese. Her CESL students bonded with her not only because Emma was charming, but also because she could connect with them through their native language. They appreciated that Emma was willing to assume the role of student at the same time as she was serving as their teacher.

Emma feels that her status as a non-native speaker of English, teaching English was definitely advantageous. Perhaps the most persuasive aspect of her role was that it demonstrated to students "that it is possible to learn a language and then teach it." She admitted to students that she sometimes made mistakes with both English and Chinese, but that mistakes were actually beneficial, an essential part of the cycle of learning a new language.

CHEROKEE AS A GRADUATE STUDENT

In 2014, Emma started to teach herself Cherokee, using smart phone applications that she downloaded from a Cherokee language website. The online class, offered by the Cherokee Nation, forces her to keep up with Native American culture, which continues to be an avid interest.

Emma started a Ph.D. in history, and later she started a Ph.D. program in education. As she felt a growing connection with education, she gave up on her history major. Her experience at the university as a French teacher and then, as an English teacher, made her realize that she enjoyed teaching. As of this writing, she is taking a Cherokee course with the Cherokee Nation, is still enrolled in Chinese classes at the Confucius Institute, and is teaching English as a second language to a wide spectrum of international students at CESL. She expects to graduate with a Ph.D. in 2018.

When reflecting on her interactions with language and culture over her lifetime, Emma returns again and again to the symbiotic relationship between them:

> What I realize is that when I choose to learn a language, it is motivated by other reasons than the language itself. I am interested in the culture, I want to understand more or lately, I want to bond with my students and understand where they come from, culturally and linguistically.

Emma believes the best way to learn a language is through immersion, which is why, in her language classes, she incorporates real-life material and authentic experiences to create an immersive experience. She says, "Immersion makes a language meaningful, and turns mastering the language into a need."

Emma still speaks French when she is on the phone with her parents, and when she returns home to France for the summer. Inevitably, while she is deep in conversation with relatives or friends in France, she will experience a pang of sadness and suddenly want to speak English, as if English were an old friend she has been neglecting for much too long.

With English, she knows that she still makes errors, but she enjoys the fact that she "can really play with the language." Emma feels like she can do what she wants in English, and, most of the time, it works. French is not as malleable. "I feel that there are limitations with French. We can create, but what we create is still considered as incorrect, maybe even a joke." With regard to structure and correctness, French is rigid and strict where English is elastic and open. Nevertheless, she loves the French language as much as she loves French culture.

Being able to express herself in so many languages enables Emma to connect with others in an intimate way. When you are a stranger in a strange land, discombobulated by the weirdness of a foreign culture and the inability to speak the language, your life can get lonely. To encounter a kind soul, someone who seems interested in you and wants to help—this is a real joy. Then, to have the kind soul speak to you in your own language—this replaces the loneliness with gratitude and hope.

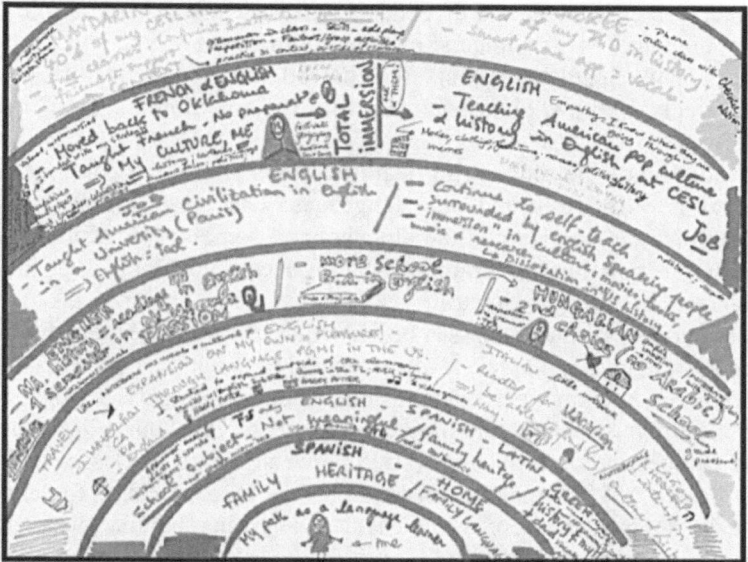

Figure 4.3   Emma's language experience, a drawing submitted for a class in 2014 to represent her language learning experience over time.

ANALYSIS

Emma's approach to language is a by-product of a greater interest in people and culture. Her interest in culture, at an early age, led her to try to master languages as a way of gaining insight into different perspectives and *different ways of being* in the world. American Pop Culture, alternatively ubiquitous, energizing, and annoying, moved her to explore the English language. She says,

> I love movies and I love to read and the music that I used to listen to and that I still listen to is primarily in English. I read a lot. I read *Harry Potter* in English at age fourteen, in middle school.

Unlike Andrew, who knew virtually no Chinese before setting foot in China, Emma had some competency with English as well as several other languages, before coming to the United States and England. Also, unlike Andrew, Emma had no epiphany wherein she miraculously transformed from a language novice to a fluent speaker seemingly overnight.

Emma was ensconced in a diversity of languages from birth and just kept adding languages, as her interest in other cultures grew. She was French by birth, but spoke Spanish to age six, then delved into French, Spanish, English, Latin, Greek, Hebrew, Hungarian, Lakota, Italian, Chinese, and Cherokee over the years.

Indeed, one of the reoccurring features of her life is the continual emergence of new interests and new languages. Last year, Emma started to learn Arabic, and she learned the alphabet and some simple words, but she promptly put a halt to her Arabic education because of the lack of time and her interest in learning Mandarin.

Emma enjoys language classes because they seem more interactive, more personal. In language classes, teachers tended to encourage her to take risks, to learn more, to extract personal meaning from assignments. In other subject areas, the emphasis was externalized, less personal, less "build-it-as-you-go."

The perspective on error also varied between language classes and other "core classes." When making mistakes in her English class, for example, Emma did not have the impression that she was wrong, but that she was in the process of working towards "right." Within the established framework of the language class, she possessed a certain autonomy, a sense of control within the limits of the experience.

Slowly, her enjoyment of learning languages extended to situations outside of school. She took hold of her own learning and started watching movies, listening to music, and reading on her own. She did not perceive her plunge into American popular culture as homework, but as a way to reproduce a state of flow.

Emma would encounter new words and expressions that she would track in her notebooks (just as Andrew did). She would work in her notebook for hours without realizing that time had passed. She would write furiously in "slow moments" while waiting in a line or taking public transportation. Emma set her own assignments and chose her own challenges.

To stay motivated, she kept amplifying the complexity of her challenges to keep up with her growing proficiency. She either pushed the language skills she had already mastered a little further or decided to start studying new languages.

At all times, she seemed to know where she was and where she wanted to be. In terms of Gardner's (1983) interpersonal intelligence, Emma would have ranked at the very top. She possessed a *metacognitive self-awareness* about her strengths, weaknesses, proclivities, and antipathies. With regard to language and culture, she seemed ever-ready to learn and to *learn for learning's sake*. She was continually focused on improving her performance.

Almost every language activity that Emma pursued, with the possible exception of Hungarian, which was a forced choice, evolved into an autotelic experience. She was going to learn the language because she wanted to learn the language.

Emma won an award for teaching language through her distinctive cultural approach and she also won an award from the state-wide Teaching English to Speakers of Other Languages (TESOL) organization. But, learning language through culture is the basic philosophy by which she has always lived—from a very young age. For Emma, the fascinating interactions between language and culture provide the grist for flow.

For human beings, thoughts inform actions, and actions inform thoughts. If a person feels enjoyment when engaging in a particular activity, the activity is more likely to be replicated than when a person engages in an activity and only feels despair. Enjoyable activities are likely to be repeated as long as they continue to be enjoyed.

As Emma started gaining mastery in one language, she promptly began exploring another language, simply as a way to keep learning interesting. As she gained confidence in her English proficiency, for example, she moved to pursuing a master's degree in Native American Studies. Then, she moved from working as instructor of French to working as a teacher of English.

Throughout her journey, Emma always heeded her internal, implicit feedback, such as when she realized that she was able to "live in English"—to function, work, and socialize in English. In a way, learning English and being functional in English was necessary to remain in flow. In order to set higher challenges, she monitored her environment, continually assessed her proficiency, and set new goals, a characteristic of the autotelic personality.

Because of the large Chinese population at the CESL where she worked, Emma became interested in Chinese culture and language. In addition to interacting with native Chinese speakers, she seized the opportunity to take free Mandarin language classes at the Confucius institute.

Emma finds flow by immersing herself in an unknown culture and continually working until she gains a certain level of autonomy in that culture. Learning a language is a micro-flow within the bigger flow activity of understanding a new culture. Repeating the experience is a means to recreating the feeling of flow.

Chapter Five

Rebecca

"I like when people say they cannot hear my American accent."

—Rebecca Borden

L1=English
L2 (fluent)=Spanish
L2 (some familiarity)=French

Rebecca is the coordinator of the First-Year Spanish program at a university, a yoga instructor, and a salsa dancer, a skill she learned after traveling to Spain in college.

Rebecca was born and raised in California in a neighborhood that was a mix of Caucasian and Hispanic. Neither of her parents spoke a language other than English, and they did not particularly value speaking another language, either. Her parents were "not very encouraging" regarding her desire to learn Spanish.

Her grandmother on her father's side was Italian and spoke Italian at home. Rebecca's father grew up hearing Italian but "never learned anything" and never spoke Italian to Rebecca or her siblings.

CHILDHOOD

Growing up in California, Rebecca had regular exposure to Spanish. In fact, her best friend in elementary school was from Mexico. According to her mother, they would come home singing songs in Spanish, or sometimes perhaps "trying to sing in Spanish." Rebecca remembers coming home and

Figure 5.1   Rebecca with her Peruvian husband Carlos and daughter Natalia whom the couple are raising as a simultaneous bilingual speaker.

trying out new words she had learned from her friend. She found it particularly enjoyable to imitate her friend's accent and tone. Rebecca attributes her early exposure to Spanish as an important factor in her mastery of pronunciation.

In fact, Rebecca's exposure to Spanish and her positive associations with the language would seem to support the *Critical Period Hypothesis* (CPH), a popular theory in the field of Second Language Acquisition that asserts that language acquisition is more natural and effective at a young age (Birdsong, 1999).

After adolescence, the subtleties of inflection and nuances of pronunciation may be much more difficult to grasp. According to the CPH, learning a language before puberty increases the chances of achieving a native-like accent. Rebecca's interest in imitation before comprehension was a boon.

"Early exposure to language, I think for me, made it so that I know how the vowels are supposed to sound, the consonants are supposed to sound like and I can enunciate them." Beyond her friendship with her Mexican–American friend, "a lot of folks in her town" in California spoke Spanish. The prevalence of the language made it easy to try out new words and phrases.

Even today, Rebecca seems to be able to easily pick up subtleties of language. Once she hears an interchange in a foreign language, she can mimic the basic sounds. "It always has been easy for me to imitate. That's what you do at the beginning when you learn a language anyways."

The first tasks in high school Spanish were to memorize words and plug them into sentences. She recalls being a good student, although she got a C in her first class because of misbehavior. She attributes her misbehavior to the dull instructional style of her Spanish teacher, whose basic approach relied upon repetition of vocabulary and memorization of rules. "We did everything a million times. I did not need a million repetitions of the same thing so I acted out." Despite her dissatisfaction with her teacher, Rebecca loved Spanish because she viewed it as a game and an excuse for fun.

"In class, I would imitate accents and goof off and make my own funny version of phrases." She emphasized that imitation of sounds and accents was something that kept her interested. Despite her ennui, Rebecca kept improving her pronunciation, which was somewhat miraculous, given that she received almost no opportunity to speak in class. She took the placement test at her college, was given some college credit based upon her performance, and was placed in an intermediate-level class.

COLLEGE

In high school, Rebecca had the impression that Spanish was "easy and enjoyable" and that her knowledge of Spanish was solid. However, after the first class of college-level intermediate Spanish, she felt lost and uncomfortable. Although her Spanish professor told her that she was good at languages and that her pronunciation was fairly accurate, she struggled. For a semester, Spanish lost some of its luster and became more like work than fun.

Then, she heard about a study abroad opportunity in Spain. She wanted to sound like a native Spanish speaker and more specifically, she wanted to sound like a Spaniard with a Castilian accent. Castilian Spanish is spoken around Madrid and is considered to be among the most prestigious Spanish dialects, higher than other versions of Spanish, such as Galician, Valenciano, or Catalan. Rebecca thought that going to Spain "was the only way I could really learn the language."

Before she went abroad, Rebecca established the goal of using the trip as a mechanism for becoming as fluent in Castilian Spanish. When she imagined herself in Spain, she visualized herself speaking at ease in a conversational manner and understanding everything that was said.

While at the university in Spain, Rebecca lived in a dormitory designated for women only, "una residencia." In her complex, there were other non-native speakers who had come to study in Spain, including three Moroccan girls, two Irish girls, and two American girls.

At the beginning of her experience in Spain, Rebecca went through a "silent period," when she did not communicate much because she "could not be Rebecca in Spanish." Because she was not sure exactly how to be friendly, funny, or sarcastic with natives without "looking stupid," she initially spent her time with the American, Moroccan, and Irish girls because they understood English and she could "be herself."

Rebecca was "too scared to talk" around natives as she was afraid of making mistakes, which was surprising, as she had always been extroverted in Spanish class. While her insecurity with the language was frustrating and depressing, it also provided her with the impetus to improve.

Rebecca started observing the phrasing and intonations of native speakers, trying to discern patterns of expression. As she did in her interactions with her Mexican friend in elementary school, "I would just experiment, try to imitate the pronunciation." She read local newspapers out loud in her bedroom to purposefully "get rid of my accent." When she would encounter new words, she would write them down and make a point of practicing them later by putting them in sentences and using them in different contexts. By imagining real situations, she retained many words by "experiencing them," even though the scenarios were always in her head.

She also looked for easy associations with her first language, English. The linguistic proximity of Spanish and English helped her to make connections among cognates in both languages. At the beginning stages of language learning, studying cognates can increase the language learner's confidence (Williams & Hammaberg, 1998). "If you can latch onto cognates, it kind of demystifies the language," Rebecca said.

Rebecca read materials almost exclusively in Spanish. As she "tried out new stuff with her Spanish roommate," she grew conscious that her level of Spanish was improving, day by day, but communicating fluently with native speakers still seemed a "big jump." Then, after four months in Spain, Rebecca "felt like I just woke up one day, and I could speak."

LANGUAGE EXPLOSION

As she described her "language explosion," she gave credit to the intensive work with vocabulary and intonation that she had pursued independently in the confines of her room and in "safe" interactions with her Spanish roommate.

She did not realize the extent of her development until she got to the point where she could bandy around words in a non-artificial way in her head. Researchers (Christoffels, Haan, Steenbergen, Wildenberg, & Colzato, 2015;

Falk, & Bardel, 2011; Gellner, & Russell, 1959; Jessner, 2003) have characterized this phenomenon as "thinking in the language," and Rebecca's ability to think in the language was fueled by her passion to become fluent.

"Maybe it was not that dramatic, but one night, I had a dream in Spanish where I was putting strings of sentences together. It just seems like my ability to speak and understand Spanish took off after the dream."

One manifestation of Rebecca's language epiphany was her seemingly "overnight" competence with formulating novel, complex sentences. The ability to be creative with the language was a key psychological turning point in her perception of her proficiency. After realizing what she could do with the language, her experience became more organically gratifying, although "it was fun already."

After her language epiphany, Rebecca found herself participating in class, asking questions, and interacting with her teacher and peers almost exclusively in Spanish. Proving to herself that she had acquired a certain degree of language competency lowered her anxiety levels, which made learning "easier."

Once Rebecca realized that she could communicate with native speakers without "overly thinking about it," the language became more enjoyable, and she was able to "be herself in Spanish." Around the time of her dream, her level of comprehension zoomed and she discovered that she could understand every phrase her roommate uttered. Rebecca's ability to "be herself" in Spanish helped her to establish a strong rapport with her Spanish roommate. "We would play our guitars and sing, and it was just really exciting."

Rebecca felt that, when she first arrived in Spain, her language limitations were significant. However, as she overcame her anxieties about her own proficiency, her stress level subsided.

Rebecca was not sure if her level of Spanish allowed her to speak more or if speaking more improved her level of Spanish, but she thought several external factors contributed to her proficiency. She realized she had to push herself to speak more, so she actively sought out activities that involved interactions with native speakers. "From month four until the end of my trip, I kind of made a mental note to spend more time in Spanish because I was going to have only one opportunity. I encouraged my English-speaking friends to speak more Spanish too."

She started hanging out with Spanish speakers, eating at restaurants with them, engaging in conversations with them, and in a more general way, living like them. She sought out a linguistic experience that was significantly more challenging, but also more gratifying. The social environment informed her language development and her language development helped her better understand the social environment.

SPANISH FLUENCY

Before going to Spain, Rebecca's original plan was to stay for a semester. At the end of the term, she had acquired a level of Spanish competence with which she was pleased, a metalinguistic knowledge of the language, and a basic understanding of Spanish customs. However, there was a feeling of incompleteness, and she realized that if she was going to leave, she might waste the chance to go even further with the language. "I thought to myself: 'Man, I am just getting started.'"

The problem was that she had arranged with her advisor to return to the university and re-enroll the following semester. Although it was not easy logistically or financially, Rebecca committed to staying in Spain for another two and a half months.

Rebecca felt like her pronunciation, in particular, improved markedly during the extra time in country. Pronunciation had been a priority for Rebecca from the very beginning of her exposure to Spanish and the extra two and a half months gave her the unrivaled opportunity to fine-tune her accent. As proof of her improvement, locals would mistake her for a native speaker upon occasion.

When reflecting on her awkward first month in Spain, grappling with the language, Rebecca considered it a "mistake" to attempt to understand every part of a sentence and the meaning of every new word because, by doing so, she instantly became inundated with too much information. Focusing on "getting everything right" obscured the gradual improvement she was making in the language and made her want to shut down rather than open up.

In retrospect, she thinks that a focus on "understanding the message being communicated" would have been a far superior strategy to worrying about "getting it right." In other words, rather than paying attention to the semantics or the grammatical structures undergirding utterances, she would have been better off concentrating on meaning. She believes that her misguided priorities significantly slowed her progress.

"Subject-pronoun and then indirect object-pronoun and then verb. Trying to process every component of a sentence rather than just having the exposure so that you begin to get a feel for what sounds right." She emphasized the importance of repetition of linguistic features and the unconscious acquisition of grammar.

Although Rebecca was happy to be home, and among friends and family, she missed aspects of her life in Spain. She started to spend more time with a group of Spanish-speaking friends who liked to salsa together. To ensure her language skills stayed current, Rebecca volunteered with the Peruvian

Student Association at the university. It was while volunteering with the Peruvian Student Association that Rebecca met one of the members whom she eventually married.

SPANISH NOW

Rebecca perceived the good language learner as someone able to make inferences. Once a learner understands inferences, progress with the language increases exponentially. "The more you know, the more you learn." When Rebecca encounters a new word in Spanish now, it does not take much effort to link it to other words she already knows.

Today one of the things she enjoys the most about speaking Spanish is how natural it has become. "I have moments where I think about the fact that I have been talking for hours in Spanish and it is just coming out like it comes out in English and it is kind of a cool feeling."

She routinely thinks in Spanish and she does not use English references as an intermediate means to understand and create meaning in Spanish. Her Spanish has become an independent system of its own. Although she views Spanish and English as being equally present in her mind, they are also reciprocal, each language deepening her understanding of the other.

Even with her incredible, native-like fluency, Rebecca admitted to still having an occasional moment of anxiety. For example, when she needed to send an email in Spanish to a celebrated Spanish academic, she asked her husband to double check the email, especially concerning tone and pragmatics.

In linguistics, pragmatics refers to the way language gives meaning to words in a certain context. Rebecca did not want to express an unintended connotation that might be inappropriate. However, now that she is married to a native speaker of Spanish, she has the opportunity to use Spanish all day, every day.

Rebecca and her husband Carlos have a little girl named Natalia. The rule of the family is for everyone to speak Spanish while inside the home, while speaking English or Spanish outside the home. While Natalia sometimes asks why she can't just "speak English all the time," the plan seems to be working as she is fluent in both languages, a simultaneous bilingual.

Before going to Spain, Rebecca had the goal of being fluent in Spanish. She wanted to converse "like a native speaker." Now that she is coordinator of a Spanish department at a major American university, her goal has evolved beyond "standards of language proficiency" into academic and professional realms.

Figure 5.2 Rebecca (far right) with friends in Medellin, Columbia. Once Rebecca made the conscious effort to shed her various anxieties about communicating in Spanish, her language skills took a quantum leap forward.

ANALYSIS

As a child, Rebecca was fundamentally a behaviorist, in that most of her creative responses were a form of imitation. She mimicked words and accents and turned the learning of Spanish into a game.

Instead of falling into a state of boredom because her high school Spanish instruction was "too easy," she created new challenges to keep the subject interesting. In terms of flow theory, she continually assessed her skill level and adjusted the difficulty of chosen tasks to match her skill level. She consistently worked to maintain an equilibrium where the task-at-hand matched her increasing ability level. That is, she strived to keep the equation, Task/ability=1 (Csikszentmihalyi, 1990).

Rebecca was initially interested in Spanish, but the challenges were not high enough, so she became bored, the state A2 explicated in table 1. As boredom is an undesirable mental state, she "modified" her experience by creating new challenges. By "acting out," as she called it, and by imitating different accents, she created her own game with its own set of rules, goals, and feedback, which allowed her consciousness to remain engaged.

This prevented her from becoming distracted and disconnected from the goal of learning Spanish. The skill she developed in connection with imitating accents is a game that falls under Caillois' (1961) category of *mimicry* (the other three categories being *Agon*, games of competition, *Alea*, games of chance, and *Ilinx*, games that alter reality).

It is entirely possible that Rebecca experienced flow "accidentally," in that she gained great satisfaction from speaking Spanish fluently, so she also took significant actions to maintain task/ability equilibrium. However, her assertive actions to increase the difficulty of her tasks seemed to have been unconscious.

An important aspect of learning and motivation is the perception of the self, the perception of the object (the language), and the perception of the "intake" of that object (learning the language). Rebecca had the impression she was not doing well because, she recognized the distance from where she was in the process of learning the language and where she wanted to be.

Setting goals is a necessary step for improvement, though goals must be attainable to enable flow. Although she was not proficient as she wished, Rebecca kept improving, which was the determining factor in her experience of learning Spanish. It was not about the level she reached but the continual

Figure 5.3 Rebecca at Machu Picchu in Peru. Rebecca notes that a critical factor in her language development was that she continually sought out immersive language environments..

march towards mastery and her own awareness of the progression. "Choosing" the right challenge required having accurate knowledge of current skills.

Traveling provides an infinite array of possible outcomes. With regard to language, traveling to an environment where the Target Language (TL) is dominant provides immediate opportunities to practice and offers continuous instant feedback. As with Emma and Andrew, Rebecca's language competence improved exponentially after becoming immersed in the environment of the TL. When she realized that she "could not be herself in Spanish," Rebecca created a new objective—to be sufficiently competent in Spanish so that conveying her personality in Spanish could be done with little effort.

Like Andrew, Rebecca tried using new words in different situations with different groups of people in an effort to make learning endure. Rebecca generated causes with the express objective of obtaining effects (feedback) so that she could gain control over her experience. In her spare time, when reading a variety of works in Spanish, she would spend hours immersed in a book without realizing that time had passed. A perception of altered time is a common effect for individuals experiencing flow.

Like Andrew, Rebecca's distinctive language epiphany occurred a little over three months after arriving in the country where the TL was spoken almost exclusively. Both Rebecca and Andrew had been cramming in their language books in their free time, creating a series of intensively focused self-administered lessons.

Rebecca explained that it was not her Spanish that had suddenly become good, but that her evaluation of her skills with the language suddenly became more accurate. While Andrew was suddenly able to understand others more readily, Rebecca was able to express herself more coherently. She was able to form complex sentences and use new vocabulary without "too much effort." As with Andrew and Emma, at the point that Rebecca was able to start being creative with the language, she transformed from a position of "learning the language" to a position of "owning the language."

Andrew's epiphany had to do with the way he understood the language, whereas Rebecca's epiphany had to do with the way she produced the language, suggesting that a "language epiphany" can take multifarious forms.

After Rebecca's "language epiphany," her motivation increased, her anxiety decreased, and she was able to perform complicated activities in Spanish, such as calling for assistance with her Internet problems or discussing the details of a meal with friends. One of Rebecca's strengths was that she was able to understand the power of the environment and to manipulate it to achieve her goals. For example, early in her visit to Spain, Rebecca became conscious of the time she spent with English speakers and recognized that the time she spent speaking English did not bring her closer to her end goal.

Asserting that Rebecca experienced flow with the Spanish language might be over-interpreting. Rather, Rebecca experienced flow while engaged in conversations with people she liked who were also speaking Spanish. When Rebecca returned from her trip to Spain, she spoke like a native. She had acquired new interpersonal skills. She could tell jokes in Spanish and understood the subtleties of Spanish cultural codes. Eventually, not only did she become a great salsa dancer, Rebecca became a salsa instructor and the coordinator of the Spanish language program at a major American university. She conducts research on language acquisition and writes academic articles in both English and Spanish. At home, she speaks only Spanish with her daughter and her Peruvian husband.

To maintain flow, Rebecca has had to go deeper and deeper into the Spanish language and culture.

Chapter Six

Genevieve

"One of the keys to learning a language is autonomy."

—Genevieve Schmitt

L1=English
L2 (fluent)=Arabic, also various dialects, such as Egyptian Arabic (EA)
L2 (some familiarity)=Latin, French

Genevieve is from Portland, Oregon, and lived there until she turned eighteen. Both of her parents grew up in the United States. Genevieve describes her mother as being a "sponge for languages" and more generally, as having influenced her love of languages. Genevieve's mother is half Assyrian and half Irish.

When in college, Genevieve's mother took extensive courses in German and spoke some French. Because of her love for languages and cultures, her mother bought phrase books and possessed "survival communication skills" in sixteen languages including Arabic, Finnish, Swedish, and Indonesian. Even today, Genevieve's mother takes classes in French and Italian.

Although not interested in languages when she was a kid, Genevieve recalls her mother emphasized the importance of education throughout her daughter's childhood. Genevieve was homeschooled until the end of her eighth grade. During Genevieve's last year of homeschooling, her mother let her pick one foreign language, a language of her choice. Although Genevieve's three older brothers, who were also homeschooled, picked Latin, Genevieve chose French. The reason she chose French was because she "loved the way it sounded." Quickly, the study of French became enjoyable.

Figure 6.1 Genevieve visits Al-Hakim Mosque in Cairo, Egypt. Genevieve's interest in Arabic was initiated by a chance encounter with a book on Arabic at her local library.

Her mother's motivation for transmitting her love for languages to her children was not intended as a practical career suggestion, but as a vehicle for helping to "expand the mind." Learning languages had brought such satisfaction to her mother that she wanted her children to experience the same kind of thrill.

Genevieve remembers having French "self-teaching books with cassette tapes," and she listened to the instructions and meticulously completed all the exercises in the book. Some exercises involved reading along with tapes and repeating phrases. During these repetitive exercises, Genevieve had fun—she was never bored. Perhaps because she tends to be systematic and structured, she liked having her own book, establishing her own goals for learning, and setting her own pace. Although she engaged in precious few creative activities with the cassette/book exercises, she felt like she made significant progress with the language.

HOMESCHOOLING

The reason Genevieve's mother chose to homeschool her children was to provide them with an education based on Christian values, as her parents were conservative Christians. Her parents wanted to make sure that the education of their children was aligned with their faith. Her mother shopped at Christian bookstores for some curricular materials. The book series chosen for French was called Powerglide.

Another reason for deciding to homeschool her children was because she had had negative experiences as a student in public schools in California, having been bullied often. Also, she viewed public schools as tending to put everyone in "the same box," regardless of talent, behavior, or potential. Homeschooling allowed Genevieve's mom to have control over the curriculum and insured that her offspring received individualized attention and customized instruction.

Before having children, Genevieve's mother taught in a private school. As a teacher, she often found herself in conflict with the head of her school for helping students who were academically behind. Her mother could not fathom the concept of schools as a train on which students had to jump. If students were not able to jump onto the train right away, they would be left behind and forgotten.

Genevieve believes her homeschool years helped her develop habits of mind that helped her approach learning from a highly disciplined perspective. One of her older bothers was homeschooled through eighth grade, while the two others were homeschooled all the way through high school. As a consequence, Genevieve's homeschooled years occurred at the same time as that of her older brothers. Because her mother was simultaneously teaching three children of different ages, Genevieve sometimes felt like "she got the short end of the stick."

Because her two older brothers were on the cusp of college, her mother was hyper-vigilant in ensuring they would be prepared. Science experiments involving labs and analysis and elaborate activities built around mathematical concepts were time consuming and usurped much of her mother's time.

While her mother was intensely supervising extended excursions into chemistry and physics, Genevieve was sometimes left to herself. Over time, Genevieve became autonomous, assertive, and independent. She did not need a teacher looking over her shoulder every second; she could do it herself.

THE PUZZLE OF LANGUAGE

In ninth grade, Genevieve entered the local public high school. She decided to continue learning French because it was "an enjoyable experience." At first, Genevieve was concerned about the transition from homeschool to public school because she wondered about what she might have missed. She discovered that some verb conjugations had not been covered by her cassettes and were unfamiliar.

However, Genevieve thought getting up to speed in French was an "exciting experience," and it did not take her long to surge to the head of the class. In fact, Genevieve did so well that her teacher recommended that she skip the second year of French to go directly to the third year.

Genevieve's third year French teacher was a native speaker who brought in authentic materials and stimulated an interest in French culture. Genevieve also took Latin, which she loved as much as she loved French. "Latin was all about the charts," Genevieve notes. Her experience with Latin involved memorizing cases and vocabulary. Although the instructor's approach to Latin was highly systematized, Genevieve thoroughly enjoyed it.

Genevieve's Latin teacher used to "hammer students" with English grammar, such as the rules for direct objects or the characteristics of subjunctive clauses, in the belief that, if students could understand the structure of English, it would be easier for them to understand the structure of Latin. While some students groaned and protested, Genevieve found that knowing the structure offered a conceptual understanding of the basic framework of language that came in handy later, especially in learning Arabic.

In fact, Genevieve claims that her Latin experience made her foray into Arabic "ten times easier." For example, she explained that, in her first year Arabic, she was exposed to "jumla ismyia" (nominal sentence, in Arabic) and "jumla fa'lyia" (verbal sentence, in Arabic). In a nominal sentence, the verb is implied and therefore it is not explicitly written. Because the "jumla ismyia" does not exist in English, it was a bit challenging to grasp. However, because of her training in Latin grammar, an implied verb "made complete sense" because it was similar to a particular case in Latin.

ARABIC

After graduating from high school, Genevieve thought she wanted to become a teacher of ancient languages. Having excelled in high school—she was valedictorian—she applied to a number of highly ranked universities. When she was not accepted into one of the most prestigious universities, she decided to attend Oklahoma Wesleyan University, a small, private college that her brother had attended and which had extended an attractive scholarship. A week before leaving for Oklahoma, Genevieve went to the library near her house and looked to see if there were any new books on the French language.

It was a small library in which one shelf was dedicated to books on foreign languages. When scanning the shelf, she found the book, *Arabic for Dummies* (Bouchentouf, 2006) and skimmed through the initial pages. It was the only book on the shelf about the Arabic language.

In her reading, she was intrigued to learn that Arabic utilized a tri-literal root system. In Semitic languages, such as Arabic, the trilateral root system is a configuration where a given word has three letters and by modifying the word, often a verb, it transforms into a noun, an adjective or other words derived from the verb. Genevieve was attracted by the logical formulation of the language's semantics.

"I just thought that was the most incredible thing I had ever seen. I did not understand why English could not do something similar because it made much more sense." There, in her small, local library, with a copy of *Arabic for Dummies* in her hands, Genevieve decided to study Arabic.

Unfortunately, Oklahoma Wesleyan University did not offer Arabic, so Genevieve majored in English and took the only language class offered, Spanish. Nevertheless, while at Oklahoma Wesleyan, Genevieve checked out books on Arabic from the library and started to teach herself the language in a very systematic way. She would draw the letters, memorize them separately, put them together in words, then repeat the process with increasingly complex words.

When her parents discovered her interest in the Arabic language, one Christmas they bought her the Rosetta Stone series in Arabic. The Rosetta Stone series prominently featured speaking and listening, and Genevieve diligently started teaching herself how to speak and understand Arabic on her own, just as she had done years earlier with her French cassettes.

After spending her freshman year at Oklahoma Wesleyan University, Genevieve transferred to another university, one widely regarded as having one of the top Arabic language centers in the world. The program, called the Arabic Flagship Program, offered an intensive, twelve-month program spent in an Arabic-speaking country, after which the student would be designated as a flagship scholar in Arabic. Genevieve was attracted to not only the program and the opportunity to go to an Arabic-speaking country, but also the flexibility of the course work. She would be able to complete a dual degree in both Arabic and Linguistics. Of course, the university also offered plenty of courses in French, in which Genevieve also enrolled.

In 2009, during the summer preceding her enrollment in the college where she would complete a dual degree, she wanted to make sure she was on track with the Arabic Flagship Program. Genevieve moved back to Portland for the summer, and while there, looked for a summer class in Arabic.

She managed to find a nearby university that offered a summer-term, intermediate-level Arabic course. Genevieve lacked the prerequisites for the class, so she contacted the professor, explained her situation, and said that she had been studying Arabic on her own. The professor advised her against taking the course in Intermediate Arabic, but offered her a deal. He would provide her with the textbook for the class and then give her a competency test. If she could manage to pass the competency test, which included a section on writing, the professor would allow her to enroll in the class.

Once Genevieve got a sense of the organization of the textbook, she devoured it. She studied about three hours every evening, at times creating flashcards and reading supplemental materials on learning Arabic. After a few weeks, the professor gave her the test, a four-hour test that ranked as "the hardest test I have ever taken." After correcting the test, the professor emailed Genevieve and asked her to visit him in his office.

He explained that her test was "full of mistakes" but that he was impressed with the amount of language she had been able to acquire in a relatively brief period of time, so he allowed Genevieve to enroll in his class. Needless to say, Genevieve earned an A in Intermediate Arabic.

FRANCE

In one of Genevieve's advanced classes in college, her French professor recommended that she go to France because she had "plateaued," and he thought that she needed an extra push to go to the next level of proficiency. Genevieve agreed, as she felt somewhat frustrated that her progress had "leveled out."

In Fall 2011, she spent three and a half months in France. Although she had been studying French for ten years prior to the trip, Genevieve still encountered difficulties when she first arrived. There was a significant gap between the French she had learned on cassettes and in school and the French she encountered in France.

When arriving in Paris, she had to quickly find her way to Bordeaux, her eventual destination, by stitching together various modes of public transportation. Simply finding her way to Bordeaux became a linguistic nightmare because people in Paris tended to speak rapidly and many had unfamiliar accents. Eventually, Genevieve found her way to Bordeaux, but not before several tribulations and frustrations.

Having arrived on French soil, Genevieve started to worry that speaking and studying in French might slow her acquisition of Arabic. To alleviate her worry, she took Arabic classes while living in France. When it came time to register for classes at Universite de Bordeaux, she discovered that she had to choose between a language track in Arabic and a language track in French; she could not take both. Genevieve chose Arabic because the Arabic classes were mainly taught in French, which would provide her with exposure to both languages in a single class.

Figure 6.2 Genevieve has a picnic with British friends in Bordeaux, France. She ended up studying Arabic in French while in France.

Nevertheless, Genevieve did not feel that she improved her Arabic skills while in France. After her French experience, she returned to Oklahoma where she was scheduled to take a test at the end of January 2012 that would determine whether or not she would go to an Arabic-speaking country. Her weakest point was speaking, and she adapted her self-teaching to incorporate more speaking. She interacted with Arabic-speaking international students and purposefully sought out every opportunity to improve her communicational skills. She met three or four times a week with an Arabic instructor for one-on-one instruction.

They started with basic conversation involving how to introduce yourself and how to talk about family, then they moved to more complex conversations, such as giving an opinion on a political issue or discussing global trends. Genevieve continued with her intensive self-teaching, incorporating new components into her "system" as she encountered them. As with the summer course in Portland, she made flashcards, and read and reviewed extensively. She describes this three-month period of intensive studying as being "a major moment" in her quest to learn Arabic. Genevieve successfully passed the qualifying exam and prepared to spend a semester in Egypt.

EGYPT

Genevieve was excited about spending a year in Egypt, as it had been in her plans since she started learning Arabic. While in the U.S., Genevieve qualified her experience as tending towards a "mechanical" and "book-based" orientation, while in Egypt, she found the language fluid and mutable. In particular, she was fascinated by the Arabic dialect spoken in Egypt, which while based on Modern Standard Arabic (MSA), differed in substantial ways. Genevieve set the goal to "sound as Egyptian as possible" and broke down her study routine into specific compartments, such as accent, intonation, idioms, and rhythm. Then, she mapped out a plan of attack and initiated the new routine.

Every day, she took MSA classes in the morning, then spent the evenings studying and preparing for classes. In between classes and studying, Genevieve simultaneously launched a campaign to learn Egyptian Arabic (EA) through interactions with locals. Unlike Andrew or Rebecca, Genevieve could point to no single language epiphany. Rather, she described her gradual mastery over MSA and EA as the result of a smooth, logical progression. Devoting afternoons and evenings to studying a language was nothing new—it had been a well-established habit for her from a very young age.

Figure 6.3   Genevieve (second from right) and friends visit the Philae Temple in Luxor, Egypt.

Eventually, Genevieve moved into an apartment with an American woman and an Egyptian woman. When the Egyptian roommate was present in the apartment, Genevieve would speak in Arabic. When outside the apartment, Genevieve would only speak Arabic. The continual exposure to the language resulted in a "skyrocketing" of fluency in both MSA and EA. One day, Genevieve realized that she was thinking almost exclusively in Arabic.

ANALYSIS

During her homeschooled years, Genevieve developed specific study habits for learning a foreign language. From an early age, she was autonomous in her work as her mother gave basic instructions, but then "let her figure it out on her own." Genevieve enjoyed the sense of control that she had over her learning. Although she admitted that the self-teaching books were highly repetitive and unsophisticated, she enjoyed being her own teacher and having responsibility for her own education.

To Genevieve, language was a puzzle, a system that could be solved if you understood how all the parts fit together. She repeatedly would work exercises, figure out where she answered incorrectly, and refine her understanding. With Latin, her structured approach was a perfect fit. The language was logical and consistent, and she could successfully apply her metalinguistic knowledge to unfamiliar words and phrases.

Genevieve experienced flow in learning a new language, but most often when exerting autonomy over what was to be learned. When goals were clear, her attention was focused, and her intensity helped her meet the current challenge—again and again. Although she lacked basic writing skills in Arabic at the time, she got approval to jump ahead to Intermediate Arabic by cramming for only a few weeks. When taking the "Arabic flagship qualifying test" that would permit her to travel to Egypt, she worked on all of her communication skills and passed the difficult exam. After arriving in Egypt, Genevieve decided that she needed to "speak like an Egyptian," so started learning EA at the same time that she was learning MSA.

Whenever feedback revealed that an aspect of her language acquisition, such as speaking or writing, was weak, Genevieve created new plans and sought out new experiences that would address the weakness. She combined "going out there" with native speakers of Arabic with studying flash cards and reading voluminously. As long as she was in control of the learning, she flourished.

Learning languages was a flow experience for her mother and her mother wanted to share that joy with her children. However, when parents share an activity they particularly love, there is no guarantee that the child will have the same kind of experience. Sometimes, if flow is experienced in the presence of language, the individual can come to associate language learning as causal. Language is only a platform where flow can be experienced. Depending on the environment, the parents' role, or the teacher's role, language learning can just as easily become a platform for anomie.

While in France, Genevieve studied French and Arabic simultaneously. In France, the Arabic instruction was in French, which made learning either language doubly challenging. Usually, learning implies acquiring a new skill by linking to a skill that one already possesses. For Genevieve, learning Arabic through French was an opportunity to compare her metalinguistic understandings of the structures of both languages.

Genevieve is a fluent speaker of Arabic and has obtained a level 3/Superior rating in Arabic via an ACTFL (American Councils on the Teaching of Foreign Languages) examination. Recently, Genevieve was selected as a Fulbright Scholar, and she will work in Jordan for several months to research Arabic dialects. She has published a chapter in a book on the topic and is quickly gaining a reputation as an authority on Arabic dialects and their myriad, complex relationship with MSA.

Chapter Seven

Scott

"Learning a language requires you to crack the code."

—Scott Mauldin

L1=English
L2 (fluent)=Spanish, French,
L2 (some familiarity)=Latin, Japanese, Chinese, German, Portuguese

Scott did not major in a foreign language, nor did he major in a field related to linguistics. Instead, Scott's initial major was Liberal Studies, and he took classes in Mandarin for a semester. But he found the courses in Liberal Studies "worthless" and switched to engineering, a field in which he remained for two-and-a-half-years.

He occasionally took humanities classes for his general education requirements and decided to pursue a minor in Spanish. Although he made good grades in engineering, he grew bored and started feeling trapped in an "uncreative, stifling program." So, he switched majors again and enrolled in International Studies. He excelled in the new field and instantly became one of the "stars" of the program, which gave him confidence that he had made the right decision.

Scott is an only child from a working class background, and he characterizes his parents as "typical blue collar workers." At the public high school, Scott hung around with "the nerdy kids." Although his friends may have been diverse, they were homogenous, language-wise and spoke only English. No one in his immediate or distant family speaks a foreign language.

Figure 7.1 Scott goes on a hike while visiting France. He contends that saturation in French for a month did far more for his language skills than "any number of years of school-based language study."

INITIAL ENCOUNTERS

In elementary school, Scott used to have a weekly Spanish class that lasted for an hour in which students learned "essentially nothing." The class was focused on basic reading, though Scott characterized the approach as "passive exposure." Despite the relative scarcity of personal interactions in Spanish, Scott learned how to count to ten and came to understand the difference between *damas* and *caballeros* (ladies and gentlemen) at the local Mexican restaurant.

However, when he tried to practice his newly acquired Spanish words with his uncle, the uncle dismissively retorted, "Next thing you know we'll be spending pesos at the dollar store!" At best, Scott's family was neutral with regard to foreign languages and, at worst, somewhat defensive about the primacy of English.

In middle school, Scott took a short "sampler" French class, which only lasted six weeks. While the class did not "teach him a lot," he learned a few silly phrases, such as, *"Comment allez-vous, une feuille de papier,"* which means, *"How are you, sheet of paper?"* The class was more like a small taste of French than a real course. The French teacher transferred to a new school after only two weeks, and the replacement did not speak French. "For all intents and purposes, I did not learn anything of note."

It wasn't until high school that Scott got seriously involved with "foreign languages" when he took Latin. In truth, because no living persons speak Latin, it is considered an ancient language, not a foreign language.

His motivation for taking Latin? "It sounded cool."

Scott considered the fact that he was trying to learn an extinct language "exotic." Studying Latin made him feel special, as most other kids took French or Spanish. An additional plus was that Latin dovetailed nicely with a growing interest in history. Scott studied Latin for two years in high school, won the award for best Latin student both years, and scored the highest grade in the school on a nationally normed test on Latin.

Scott's success in Latin had a positive effect on his disposition towards languages. His teachers and fellow students "put into my head the idea that I was good at languages."

Another moment that Scott perceives as a turning point in his language learning experience is a book he read in high school entitled *The Unfolding of Language* by Guy Deutscher (2005). An introduction to linguistics intended for a nonlinguistic audience, Deutscher's book examines different inflections in Latin, the influence of Latin on romance languages, and the tendency of languages to evolve over time. Scott thought the lessons of the book were revelatory, particularly with regard to structure and language change.

When Scott entered college, he did not know Spanish but had a girlfriend at the time who spoke Spanish fluently. She was Caucasian, but had taken Spanish in middle school and was enrolled in Advanced Placement Spanish in high school. This romantic relationship motivated Scott to learn Spanish so that he could "keep up with her."

During his first semester of college, Scott studied Spanish on his own. In his free time, he would write down structures and vocabulary and try to apply them immediately. For example, when he learned the progressive tense in Spanish, he would start with a "doodling sentence like, *estoy escribiendo en español"* (*"I am writing in Spanish"*). He practiced everything repetitively and made sure that he knew how to use the new phrase in a "live" situation.

Scott also practiced with his girlfriend because they had developed a lively rapport. His level of proficiency in Spanish zoomed and, after only a few weeks, speaking Spanish seemed "natural." Scott attributes the ease with which he learned Spanish to a combination of factors:

1. His "passive exposure" to Spanish at a very young age,
2. The prevalence of Spanish around him (not only his girlfriend, but lots of other Spanish speakers, too),
3. His background in Latin.

The first two factors allowed him to become familiar with Spanish phrases as *"Donde esta el baño?"* (*Where is the bathroom?*) His experience with Latin gave him the background, necessary to understand verb conjugations and to decode many vocabulary words "very naturally." Scott watched movies in Spanish and read some Spanish literature, such as poems by Pablo Neruda, just to ascertain how much he could understand.

Scott decided to take a placement test to see if he could get some credit for his budding Spanish proficiency. However, after taking the placement test, he realized that his level of proficiency was not where he wanted it to be. As a result, he decided to "jump into Spanish studying headfirst."

He bought flash cards and grammar books, and for a period of a little over two weeks, he spent his free time studying Spanish. He memorized vocabulary, studied grammar, and conversed in Spanish as much as his girlfriend could tolerate. As with previous language mavens highlighted in this book, Scott considers this intensive studying period as crucial in the evolution of his Spanish proficiency.

"I'd say there was a two or three week explosive growth period in which all the vocabulary and grammar sort of congealed into something I could use to actively communicate with Spanish speakers."

Scott's subsequent score on the Spanish placement test gave him credit for Spanish I, II, and III, not bad for someone who had never taken a Spanish course in college. After the placement test, Scott felt a certain sense of gratification, so he relaxed a bit. Since he was going to be taking Spanish IV the following semester, he had little incentive to continue with his maniacal cramming. As a result, Scott's level of Spanish "plateaued."

JOURNEYS

The summer that followed Spanish IV, Scott decided to journey to Guadalajara, Mexico for about a month. When Scott arrived, he discovered that his academic knowledge of grammar and composition were good, but he lacked the linguistic dexterity to communicate in Spanish with native Mexicans. His Mexican host mother was soft-spoken and did not say much. Scott had gone to Mexico with a group of university students who often preferred to speak in English, so his interactions with the Spanish language were limited, despite being in Mexico.

Because Scott was shy and "not a partier," he declined invitations to go to bars or clubs with Mexican students. He remembers being absolutely paralyzed by not knowing whether to address someone as *tú* or *usted* (informal vs formal *you*) and "would go out of my way to avoid making sentences that would force me to try one of them."

When he came back to the university, he enrolled in Spanish V and in Spanish VI. The following summer, he went to Spain for a month to work at the American Embassy. His first day in Spain, Scott had to make phone calls in order to find an apartment. Talking on the phone in another language was a skill with which he had had no experience.

Working at the embassy continually placed him in uncomfortable positions. He had to arrange and conduct meetings with Spanish government officials, interview them, and compile their responses into a report. He had to attend conferences, had to listen to lectures, and had to "learn to *schmooze* in Spanish." He was forced to be meticulous and precise with what he said and did.

He spent time with many exchange students from around the European Union, and they spoke almost exclusively in Spanish. While the academic

Figure 7.2 Forced completely out of his comfort zone in Madrid, Spain, Scott (far left) bonded quickly with a group of students and lost his inhibitions about speaking the language.

level of Spanish may not have been particularly high, he felt little reticence about speaking Spanish among this group of friends, many of whom were learning Spanish as an L2 just as he was.

In Spain, Scott overcame the apparent aversion to speaking Spanish that manifested in Mexico. Because of the dual nature of his language learning in Spain—professional during the day, casual at night—he came to be the most polished speaker among his group of friends, and one of the most fluid speakers of Spanish at the embassy.

After three months, Scott took a trip alone to the south of the country—Cordoba and Granada. Navigating bus stations, asking directions in a strange city, buying things in stores all by himself was an exhilarating experience that gave Scott a deep sense of satisfaction.

NEW CHALLENGES

After Scott's return from Spain, the entire Modern Language department knew he had been abroad, and the Spanish instructors began conversing with him in Spanish. He had many long conversations in Spanish with a Mexican–American coworker. He read research in Spanish for his classes whenever he could. His positive experiences with Spanish and Latin soon triggered an interest in other foreign languages such as Japanese, Chinese, and French.

With regard to Japanese, Scott qualifies his initial interest as "dabbling," as opposed to "studying." His goal with Japanese was to become functionally communicative. Just as in the beginning stages of his learning Spanish, learning Japanese became his "primary form of entertainment."

At some point, he ordered Rosetta Stone in Japanese and studied it by himself for three weeks. Part of his motivation was that he had two friends who were also studying Japanese. His plan was to "go home, lock himself in his room, and pop out after three weeks, try to communicate with them, and surprise them."

Scott became convinced he had an ability to demystify language, and he had an internal drive to prove it to himself again and again. He believed that demonstrating his knowledge of the "hidden code" of language had to be validated by others. However, impressing his friends was never the only goal. Scott simply found gratifying the process of "decoding" the structure, extracting the basic concepts, and speaking a new language in real-life situations.

Scott would spend six hours every day memorizing new Japanese vocabulary, learning new grammatical structures, and trying to apply them in his writing. Although it was an intensive schedule, Scott explained that he would get "perverse pleasure" out of dedicating a specific allotment of time towards the sole goal of becoming competent in Japanese.

Incredibly, Scott became "communicatively competent" in Japanese in a matter of weeks, but unfortunately his two friends studying Japanese soon graduated and took jobs elsewhere. Scott explains that he did not actually "stop" learning Japanese, but that opportunities to practice Japanese became so scarce that he lost interest.

For Scott, learning a language has much in common with learning to play the piano. When trying to learn the piano, he deconstructed the skills necessary to play—fingering, timing, touch—and then tried to reproduce them, but he found it difficult to discern his progress, which is why he stopped playing the piano. However, when learning a language, Scott felt as if he could see immediate progress, which kept him engaged.

When he played the piano, he did not feel like he was getting better, so he quit. With languages he could "go back the next day and read over the things that I tried to do the day before" and observe his improvement. Self-perception and self-regulation were absolutely necessary for him to acquire a new skill. "It is the feeling of instant gratification and instant self-edification that I get when I learn a language that keeps me going."

"Sometimes I'll have a bike riding spell or a baking spell, or other times I'll have a language spell." To him, these different spells depend on his mood at a certain point and on "what else is going on in my life."

FRENCH

Scott divides his encounters with French into two phases. In the first phase, which he calls, "French for Flair," he just played around with the language. In high school, he found an online paper about the avian flu written in French. When reading the paper, he realized that he was able to understand most of it. As a result, he started trying to reproduce the language by practicing random, often silly phrases, regardless of accuracy or meaning.

Today, Scott describes his high-school knowledge of French as artificial. "I thought I knew French because I could read a paper and understand most of it, but I did not realize that academic terms use a high incidence of cognates between English and French."

In the second part of his French experience, which he calls "Intense French," he became an active learner. To launch his study, Scott used some of the same processes he utilized in learning Spanish and Japanese. He purchased flashcards and a dual-language book, which had French on one page and English on the other.

He would first read the French to see what he understood, then make notes on words that he did not know. He continually self-assessed to determine his next steps. He started working with a coworker who was studying French and perceived his several hours with his friend as having a positive influence on his commitment.

He purchased *Le Petit Prince* by Antoine de Saint-Exupéry, a popular 1943 novel for children, and started reading it, inferring meaning and trying to see how much he knew. Scott's motivation was purely intrinsic, "for fun." He learned French in relation to three languages he already knew—English, Spanish, and Latin. "The way I learned French I would say is not as a discrete language but … as how it was different from Spanish and Latin."

For example, when faced with the *passé composé* (simple past) in French, Scott would apply concepts he learned from Spanish and Latin to French inflections. He would repeat this methodology wherever possible. In other words, he would "learn what he already knew" about the language by "mutating Spanish and Latin into an ability to communicate in French."

Another determining factor that helped Scott commit to French on a long term basis was his acquaintance with a new French teaching assistant named Emma, who arrived in the department of Modern Languages in 2013. Emma came from France to pursue a degree in Native American History and, subsequently, in World Languages. Scott asked her for help with his French because she seemed "nice and personable in many ways."

When they spent time together, Scott realized that it was an opportunity to put into practice his countless hours of cramming with books and flashcards. Although he would still have brief conversations at work in French with coworkers and students, he practiced every day with Emma.

After they started to hang around with each other more and more, one day, Emma admitted that she was impressed by Scott's level of proficiency in French. He told her he had never taken a French course, that he was self-taught. Scott was delighted that a girl that he liked seemed impressed by his language skills. "That was useful," Scott says. Once they started dating, their mutual interest in languages was both a gift and a point of contention.

On the positive side, they could discuss a variety of languages and could share their innumerable observations on language, thought, and culture. On the negative side, Scott was consumed with French when Emma was looking for more opportunities to speak English. French is not something that Emma was keen on practicing too much, although she loves her language. Scott explains, "She wanted to speak English all the time, and I wanted to speak anything but English."

CRYSTALLIZATION

When studying a language, Scott would learn "bits of the language" and put them (or try to put them) directly into practice. It was not easy to put everything into practice as it depended on outside factors such as context, topic, and difficulty of the words used during conversations.

After a month of hanging around with Emma, Scott was able to put most of what he had learned into practice, along with new aspects of the language he was learning every day. He started to understand how aspects of the language fit together to create functional communication. Scott termed the process of learning a language *crystallization*:

> When I refer to crystallization, I'm thinking about the crystallization of a supersaturated solution wherein all the particles are jam-packed and eager to cling to something and need only a nucleus on which they can all fall into place. I think the analogy is apt for my experience with French because I felt "supersaturated" with my prior knowledge and vocabulary and just needed the opportunity for that knowledge to precipitate out into a useful form.

Scott explained that his biggest problem was that his French was not academic but literary and heavily influenced by Spanish. For example, he would use phrases like "*Il ne m'importe pas*" and Emma would correct him and tell him that French people say "*je m'en fiche*" or "*peu m'importe.*" All three expressions mean "I don't care," but Scott's utterance was a literal translation from Spanish. Indeed, Scott's French even sounded Spanish.

Crystallization also happened with idiomatic expressions and with grammatical structures. For example, when using the French simple past, one might say, "*Tu as pas mangé*" (literally "you have not eaten"), but such a formulation is not possible in Spanish "(*Tu) no has comido.*" What Scott explains with these kinds of examples is that he needed to make specific mistakes to enable him to remember how the structure of French aligned (or failed to align) with Spanish.

In summer 2014, Scott travelled to France for the first time to meet Emma's parents and stayed for a month. When he first arrived, he described his level of French as functional, but, after a month, he observed significant improvement.

When comparing his intensive "alone time" studying French and his experience in France, Scott did not qualify his time in France as being "better"—just different. He felt that he would not have improved as much had he not spent countless hours with flash cards and continually conversing with Emma.

During his three weeks of cramming, his learning was more internal and personal: a lot of "textual reading, mental production, and pronunciation." He worked on his oral delivery in French during solitary times and when he was with his girlfriend. Before going to France, he perceived his strong points to be reading, writing, and pronunciation. Despite his progress, sometimes he had difficulties understanding when French people other than his girlfriend spoke.

After a week or two in France, Scott experienced a "second crystallization" around his listening skills. While he performed well in a direct one-on-one conversation, he had difficulty focusing on multiple speakers. However, one day, while participating in a conversation with multiple speakers, he noticed his "most poignant crystallization moment ever." After his second crystallization, Scott felt like his listening comprehension "jumped from 40% to 80%."

Scott first perceived the phenomenon of crystallization as being divided into the four primary skills of language: speaking, writing, reading, and listening. He had experienced crystallization in the first three skills when he was still in the United States because he had consistent, relevant, ample opportunities to practice them.

In addition, he experienced crystallization in listening while being in France through interactions with native speakers. After a month in France, Scott had to think less and less before speaking in French. Today, Scott has casual conversations in French with his girlfriend and her family on Skype or on the phone without thinking much about it.

PERCEPTION OF LANGUAGES

Given that his parents are not "language people at all," Scott mainly attributed his success to a demystification of the language. He managed to overcome the canard that language learning was a painful and difficult process. Once Scott accepted that proficiency was due to the amount of time spent learning, mastering a language no longer seemed insurmountable. "It's only a matter of time. It's not like I lack the skills or the mental faculties. I can do it if I put the time into it."

The skills he referred to are the metalinguistic strategies he had developed while learning different languages. Although his fluency in French was impressive, Scott asserts that the reason for his proficiency was the expenditure of adequate time and effort. However, with Chinese, he just "did it for fun" and had no reason to go much beyond basic communication skills.

Today, Scott might spend an hour here and there doodling with German or Portuguese "just to try to see the way they work." With regard to methodology, Scott approached every language the same way. "I begin with grammatical structures, going at it from a linguistic perspective. I look at it like a system. So, if I understand how the structure is created, I can learn the vocabulary to put into it."

Grammars provides a template in which he plugs in different vocabulary words. Before memorizing vocabulary, Scott tries to understand the grammar of a language in relation to other languages. Rather than viewing French as a system, Spanish as a system, and so forth, he perceives language as one big system that is divisible into smaller inter-related subsystems. If Scott can understand the "internal logic of the language, then I can improve quickly."

One of the reasons Scott has a mania for his method is because he wants to avoid embarrassment. As a speaker of English, Scott perceives himself as having good diction, being articulate, and communicating with competence. When he starts learning a foreign language, he loses these strengths because he lacks the linguistic knowledge to be competent in an unfamiliar language. So, he spends hours at first cramming alone. He does not want to reveal himself as lacking in his ability by incorrectly communicating his thoughts. This fear of embarrassment motivates him to learn "the right way" one step at a time.

As a result, Scott finds unappealing, the idea of going to a foreign country without first knowing the language. Rather than struggle with the language and show how much he does not know, Scott would probably avoid communicating altogether. Intensive self-study is a necessary first step that allows him to skip the "embarrassment period" and launch more readily into communicative competence.

Scott wants to be right the first time. For example, before speaking in public, he would check online and look at different usages of a word to make sure that his usage fit the context. When he is wrong, Scott feels "horrible" and tends to shut down. "I prefer to correct myself privately and not reveal my weaknesses to people."

When first meeting a native speaker of a language he is learning, Scott "would think the sentence a thousand times in my head to make sure I will say it correctly" because he wants to make a first good impression. *A good impression* is actually a goal that he seeks to achieve when interacting with a native speaker.

Although Scott describes himself as a risk-averse introvert, he contends that his discomfort and anxiety over making mistakes actually enhance his motivation.

THE GAME

While trying to "decode" French, Scott realized that it was not the same as decoding Japanese. As French is closer to Spanish, it was logical that he could use his previous knowledge of Spanish and modulate it to enhance his learning of French. However, as he improved in French, he did not need the Spanish "training wheels" after he achieved a basic level of competence. With Japanese and Chinese, the structures of the languages were different. According to Scott, learning a language is a game:

> To a certain extent, it is definitely a game-like mentality. I think that's a very strong analogy. If you play a game for a week and come back at the first level, you think, "*My gosh, this is so easy, how did I ever get confused about this!*"

With language, it's often the same, but the extent to which one can view a language as a code-like system is highly dependent on the language family and structure of the language. Japanese, for example, functions very much like a programming language such as Java. In Java, you might say "string Name = 'Scott'," which means you are declaring a variable "Name," declaring it as a string (a line of text) and setting it equal to "Scott."

In Japanese you would say *watashi no namae wa Scott desu* to mean "my name is Scott," and you do that by putting the first person pronoun, *watashi*, setting it to the possessive state by adding the *no*, invoking "name" and setting it to subject (*namae* and *wa*, respectively), and then completing the equation as "=Scott," in this case *Scott desu*. To look at it again in Java syntax, *Possessive I Subjective Name* = *"Scott."*

Chinese, in contrast, does not function like an object-oriented programming language, and is often compared to "Lego." As in English, word order determines meaning and, like German, small words can combine into larger accumulations for more complex meaning. In either case, or in any language in between, learning the syntax and morphology is the skeleton of the language and what truly makes a language, aside from the culture, unique from another. After one understands the syntax and morphology, the rest is mostly vocabulary and practice.

Scott conceptualizes languages under a single category of linguistics. In pursuing the study of languages in this manner, Scott is able to approach any language from the perspective that he already possesses significant background knowledge on it.

ANALYSIS

Scott's successful experience with language is fascinating, in part, because Scott does not perceive himself as a "language person." As opposed to the five other individuals featured in this book, Scott did not major in languages nor in any field related to linguistics. Rather than approaching language from a socio-cultural or performative perspective, Scott's approach is analytical. He views language as a system and focuses his energies on understanding its deep, indelible structure.

Scott underwent a process of trial-feedback-validation as he began to develop his own approach to learning a language, an approach not universal, but personal, intense, and continually probing. Learning involves establishing a connection between the self and the object to be learned—the language.

When learning Spanish, Scott would memorize sentences as chunks, such as *"Donde esta el baño?"* (*Where is the restroom?*). In Second Language Acquisition (SLA), this formulaic approach to language learning would seem to adhere to a highly behaviorist orientation. In the late 1950s, Skinner developed an approach to learning that treated knowledge as behavior, that is to say, a "stimulus–response" approach.

By repeating specific sentences over and over, Scott's first approach to language allowed him to possess basic skills to express certain ideas in the target language. The behavioristic approach has limits, and the technique did not prepare Scott to go to the next step, which is being creative with the language.

As he improved in Spanish, Scott reached a point in which he plateaued, mainly because there was no incentive to continue his quest towards mastery. Again, the only way to develop increasingly sophisticated skills is to encounter challenges just beyond our reach. By traveling to Spanish-speaking countries, such as Mexico and Spain, Scott kept increasing the complexity of the task-at-hand.

He described the process of learning a language as "a staircase, a punctuated equilibrium of plateau and improvement." The plateau abruptly ended when he was exposed to new challenges that required incrementally higher expenditures of psychic energy.

Traveling abroad provides a language learner with an array of challenges, but it also permits a great deal of autonomy in the formulation of potential responses. While successful language learners acquire a knowledge of new words and phrases, they also acquire a better understanding of how a language is learned.

Scott set challenges that were contingent upon language availability, potential rewards, and the social context. The goals he set for himself with Spanish were not the same as for Japanese. His goal with Japanese was to decode the language, achieve communicative competence within weeks, and awe his friends.

Being able to decode the language, extract concepts, and reapply them provided him with a sense of control over the experience. It was the ability to be creative with the language combined with immediate feedback that provided a sense of engagement and, eventually, satisfaction.

Scott created learning opportunities that tested his skills and, once his skills were validated, he was able to move to the next step. Scott was continually active while learning; never passive. Scott was the subject of his experience rather than the object, though he was a self-proclaimed risk-avoider.

Scott's interest in French came after his having reached a certain level of proficiency in Spanish. "The way I learned French I would say is not as a discrete language, but I began learning French as how it was different from Spanish and Latin." It is not uncommon for bilinguals of Spanish and English to "play with French."

Among the individuals featured in this book, at least three, Rebecca, Scott, and Emma, showed an evolution in their perception of languages. Little by little, they started perceiving languages in a more holistic manner. All languages became *one language* rather than *many languages*. This perception of the universe of languages as a single linguistic entity was most acute in Scott.

In addition to a natural curiosity about languages and a perceived "talent" for languages, Scott also had external factors to push him along—his girlfriend and her opinion of his prowess in French, the journey to France to meet his girlfriend's parents. What is interesting about Scott's foray into French is his autodidactic drive, his unwavering discipline to master languages.

Perhaps indeed, his greatest achievement is that he created a rigorous, relentless schedule that led to mastery of French. As Csikszentmihalyi explains, taming one's use of time is essentially exerting control over the self.

In Scott's free time, he would choose his own goals, set his own challenges, and through a self-sustaining system of trial and error, would find the stimuli that matched his skills so that he could sustain a state of flow. Did Scott's ability to tame time promote flow, or does being in a state of flow enable time management? Perhaps both ideas are valid, a dialogic circle in which the individual jumps from one end to another.

After reading Deutscher's *Unfolding of Language*, after experiencing language learning in multiple languages, Scott developed a metalinguistic sense about languages. He describes the process as the *language game*, a contest in which he defined the rules, structure, assessment, values, and goals for learning.

In other words, Scott repeatedly played the game of language because it put his mind into a state of flow. For Scott, flow involved finding out how languages work; deconstructing a concept into tangible parts, then reconstructing the system while testing for different outcomes. A good illustration is the way Scott unconsciously adopted Grimm's Law in his language learning experience. Grimm's Law is the group of rules that govern changes between Romance and Germanic languages.

For example, the letter *p* in a Romance language would translate as *f* in a Germanic language. Hence, in Latin *pesc-* would be *fish* in English. Another similar rule is that in Romance words of Germanic origin that begin with a *g*, the English equivalent would be a *w*, as in *guerre/war*, *guêpe* (from *guesp*)/ *wasp*, *garde/ward*, and *Guillaume/William*. According to Scott, "knowing rules like these allows an instant, rapid expansion in one's vocabulary in a target language."

Scott adopted an *engineer's* approach to language, which accessed language from the inside, from the perspective of a language's structure, its bare bones. In this view, for Scott, French was just another variation of an Indo–European language, and the Subject-Verb-Object pattern was common in Indo–European languages. Scott viewed all languages from this perspective, as a system to be understood, solved, and mastered.

Conclusions

How the five individuals in this book—Andrew, Rebecca, Emma, Genevieve, and Scott—pursue fluency in a language is fascinating in light of their individual stories. As they reflected on their experiences to gain an understanding of what worked and what didn't, their experiences can be considered *in toto* to assess optimal language learning.

At some point, all five language mavens started at point zero, but managed to achieve not only competence but mastery over one or more languages.

From a desire to travel and see the world, Andrew moved from knowing nothing about Chinese to becoming a fluent, certified teacher of Chinese. From a spark of fascination with American culture, Emma eventually became a multilingual teacher of English in America. From a random encounter with a book about the Arabic language at her local library, Genevieve moved from not understanding a single Arabic letter to becoming an authority on Arabic dialects. From a passing interest in the orderliness of Latin, Scott transformed into a masterful polyglot. How did they do it?

Examining their language acquisition strategies collectively yields nine lessons:

1. The environment is critical
2. Periods of intensive study are foundational
3. The learner should exert control over the experience
4. A language epiphany will come
5. The urge to merge is natural and beneficial
6. An interest in life precedes an interest in language
7. There is no single path to fluency
8. Flow is subjective
9. Flow amplifies language learning

1. THE ENVIRONMENT IS CRITICAL

Clearly, the environment plays a key role in the learning of languages (Krashen, 1976; Krashen, 1977). For example, it is more difficult to learn Chinese in a rural area of the United States than it is from an apartment near Beijing Normal University. Andrew spent four years in China. Although he started out thinking he would just learn the minimum amount of Chinese, his fluent friend and his drive to communicate and understand the "people in the street" drove him to master the language.

Rebecca spent time in various countries where Spanish was the dominant tongue, including Mexico, Spain, and South America. She married a native Spanish speaker and lived in a state with an abundant population of Spanish speakers. Emma, who is French, lives in a country where one of her target languages (TLs)—English—is the dominant language. Because Emma has a fascination with Native American culture, she has unique access to Native American languages, such as Lakota and Cherokee.

Genevieve studied French and Arabic in the United States and journeyed across the country to enroll in an Arabic flagship program. From there, she spent time in France and then went to Egypt for a year to study Arabic.

Scott taught himself Spanish in high school so that he could converse with his Spanish-speaking girlfriend. Eventually, Scott went to Spain where he had repeated, intensive interactions with native Spanish speakers as a representative of the U.S. Embassy. When he returned from his trip, the professors in the Spanish Department at his university all started speaking Spanish to him.

Scott also learned French on his own. Then, he met his French girlfriend, and they frequently conversed in French. He went to France, met his girlfriend's parents, who spoke no English, and stayed at their home.

Beyond the environmental availability of the language in terms of quality and quantity, crosslinguistic factors have a tremendous impact on learning. The structure of a language, the learner's current level of proficiency and attitude, and the order in which someone has encountered languages influence the speed and effectiveness with which a new language is mastered.

While Andrew initially wanted to be conversant in Chinese, Rebecca wanted to attain a perfect Castillian accent, which she achieved. From a crosslinguistic point of view, the distance between Spanish and English is much less than the distance between Chinese and English. During initial stages of language acquisition, the learner relies heavily upon background language as a structure for understanding the new language. When the TL has little in common with the L1, the degree of difficulty dramatically increases (Lindqvist, 2009).

At the beginning stages of learning, Andrew and Rebecca both spoke only one language, English. Thus, their background language helped determine the nature of the challenges they faced with the TL. Because English and Spanish are close Indo–European languages, Rebecca already possessed a "headstart" in her acquisition of Spanish. However, Andrew's knowledge of English did little to help him master Chinese.

2. PERIODS OF INTENSIVE STUDY ARE FOUNDATIONAL

All five individuals shared these traits:

1. They purposefully and expertly designed extended periods of independent study.
2. They possessed an implacable discipline that enabled them to focus penetratingly on aspects of the TL for hours at a time.
3. They showed remarkable similarities in organization, knowledge of the self, knowledge of content, and knowledge of the nature of the interaction of the self with the content.
4. Studying solo was an end in itself. That is, the process of striving to master the language was autotelic.

In every case, undertaking the task of studying intensively was necessary for each to maintain flow in pursuit of the TL (Rubin, 1975; Tardy & Snyder, 2004).

When Scott was learning French at first, his motivation was intrinsic, as he expected no particular reward from learning the language. He just thought it "sounded cool." However, when cramming in Spanish, Scott's motivation was to make a good score on a placement test that would give him college credit and place him in an advanced level of Spanish (though he had taken zero college Spanish courses).

Although this type of motivation was external, Scott organized his time and set up goals that he turned into a series of internal challenges. This self-created series of mini-challenges furnished him with the necessary feedback loop to keep going.

So, although Scott began studying Spanish in a way that was not "flow friendly," in that his motivation was external, he created a plan of self-study that made flow possible. He admitted that he would not have studied Spanish if not for a placement test. So, Scott transformed the "imposed" experience into a process under his control.

When Rebecca was learning Spanish in high school, her motivation was extrinsic, as her interest in the course was wholly correlated to the expectation of a grade. Although the class was boring, she continually enhanced the complexity of the experience through games involving misbehavior, imitating accents, playing around with new words, and otherwise embellishing the rudimentary assignments given to her.

An individual's initial motivation and the probability of achieving a state of flow are closely related, though independent. Motivation does not determine flow, but flow is more likely to occur when a person is motivated (Xiaowei, 2013). From the evidence of the experiences of Andrew, Emma, Rebecca, Genevieve, and Scott, apparently a state of flow can arise from activities that are not intrinsically motivating.

For example, a person who hates trying to learn vocabulary may not be intrinsically motivated to study, but feels compelled to do so for a forthcoming vocabulary exam. However, if the act of studying can be transformed into a flow experience by customizing it to suit particular goals and personal predilections, then flow becomes possible.

To maintain adequate levels of psychic energy for the task-at-hand, the challenge must always be suitably difficult as well as somewhat attractive (Roy, 1960). All the language mavens set up schedules, made lists of words to acquire, set deadlines, and actively and continually *monitored* their learning.

3. THE LEARNER SHOULD EXERT CONTROL OVER THE EXPERIENCE

The metaknowledge that is developed about language learning empowers an individual to exert a certain amount of control over the experience. An individual must accurately assess what she/he knows, as well as understand the possibilities available in the environment. Being able to determine "the next step" was a talent that was repeatedly demonstrated.

Vygotsky's (1978) zone of proximal development (ZPD) provides an apt construct for the ways learners acquire a language. However, for someone to "get into the zone," requires adequate exposure and opportunity. Rather than settle for the stimuli that is easily accessible, the successful language learner actively seeks out new experiences. If the experience is not readily available, he/she creates it, often in the confines of a sparsely decorated room in a foreign land. Successful language learners often are their own best teachers.

A conscious effort to use the language creatively seems to be a crucial step. Each pointed to the moment of *creative transfer* as key. Creative transfer, although subjective, affected not only proficiency, but also the intensity and duration of flow.

In every case, the individual analyzed the input they were exposed to, extracted lessons from the input, committed the lessons to memory, and subsequently applied what was learned to novel situations. At some point, all five language mavens suddenly discovered that they were able to form sentences and phrases they have never previously heard. As Chomsky's Universal Grammar suggests, memory and creativity are at the heart of language learning. It is only by recognizing new concepts and understanding how they relate to current skills that the learner can grow.

Of course, exposure to a phenomenon does not necessarily mean anything was learned. In second language acquisition (SLA), the difference between exposure and learning is captured by the term *intake*. *Input* is exposure, and *output* is the content produced by the learner as a result of the intake. *Intake* is the knowledge actually acquired through experience, which is connected to previous knowledge.

By being able to apply previously acquired concepts to new experiences, the language mavens used the universality that undergirds language to reapply broad concepts to particular situations. The language mavens were not always correct when applying what they thought were inductively-vetted rules and concepts, but formulating these new ideas involved sophisticated analysis and creative thinking, which significantly enhanced their understanding of how the language works.

By using repetition, multiplying experiences, and continually increasing exposure to the TL, language mavens engaged in a continual process of confirmation and contradiction. For example, when Andrew used Chinese accurately while shopping in China, obtaining the item he asked for provided him with the necessary feedback to let him know he was on the right track. In speech act theory, the utterance of a question is a performative activity.

When a phrase is enunciated, it alters the reality by performing an action, which in the case of a language learner, provides valuable feedback to the performer of the utterance. When asking a question to the shopkeeper, Andrew received instant feedback. The constant availability of feedback contributed to his feeling of control over the experience and provided a palette for creative action.

A recurrent impression among language mavens was a feeling of playing a game (Klabbers, 2000). Rebecca felt anxiety during her first weeks in Spain, a common occurrence among language learners (Horwitz, 2001). But, as Rebecca improved the quality of her intensive studying, she acquired the necessary skills to meet the challenge of fluency, which initially appeared to be out of reach. After experiencing an epiphany (what she termed a *language explosion*), her disposition towards Spanish shifted from anxiety to playfulness.

As Rebecca did throughout her language journey, she transformed the stressors around language acquisition into a lighthearted game. At some point, all of the language mavens referred to their quest to master a language as a kind of game. No two "games" were alike, as they were created to suit the perceptions, skills, and idiosyncrasies of the individual.

Scott's game was to deconstruct a language and to analyze it as an autonomous system, detached from the culture or place it represented. Scott was convinced that every language has an underlying structure and that, once the code was cracked, learning the language would become far simpler. Once Scott "cracked the code" of one language, he promptly moved to another one. Studying a new language was a way to recreate the sense of flow that he enjoyed from the process.

At times, Scott was more interested in cracking the code than in actually learning the specifics of a language. However, make no mistake—his pronunciation, phrasing, knowledge of vocabulary, and language sensibilities were impeccable.

4. A LANGUAGE EPIPHANY WILL COME

Andrew termed the seminal moment in his learning of Chinese as an *epiphany*. A similar sense of breakthrough occurred for all participants. Scott described the moment as a *crystallization*, Rebecca referred to it as an *explosion*, Genevieve called it a *skyrocketing*, and Emma viewed it as a *gestalt* or a *"knitting together."*

From the perspective of flow theory, little discrete activities, which had heretofore provided several states of mini-flow, came together to create a momentous "tipping point." While Rebecca was still working on her Spanish accent, she started to intensively study grammar and vocabulary, two separate, but related areas. Once she reached a certain proficiency in both grammar and vocabulary, these skills began to emerge in her daily, oral interactions in Spanish. Eventually, walls between categories melted away and she suddenly became aware of their unified interdependence.

As Emma was improving her English, she was also developing expertise in Native American literature, language, and history. As she connected her new knowledge with her burgeoning skills, she experienced a gestalt, where the sum of her learning became greater than the accrual of each of the parts.

Epiphanies involved a definite sensation of letting go, as if some subconscious force momentarily emerged to take over the language processing duties of the brain. Although the use of language is voluntary and conscious, when they slid into fluency with native speakers, language mavens felt as if "everything came together" without any conscious effort, at least most of the time. Inevitably, the feeling of crystallization occurred during a state of flow, when the challenge was quite high, but a concerted effort in a short amount of time helped give the mind the tools necessary to meet the individual's goals.

A natural by-product of fluency is the development of metalinguistic knowledge and metalinguistic intuition, which helps build increasingly sophisticated and powerful thought processes (Ringbom, 1987). These enhanced thought processes are not merely hypothetical—neuroscientists have validated physical changes in the brain as the result of purposeful manipulation of the environment.

Researchers in neuroscience long ago discovered that "every part of the nerve cell from soma to synapse alters its dimensions in response to the environment" (Diamond, 1988, p. 156). Pribaum (1991, p. xxii) writes that "brain processes undergo a dynamic matching procedure until there is a correspondence between the brain's microprocessors and those in the sensory input."

5. THE URGE TO MERGE IS NATURAL AND BENEFICIAL

When improving skills and facing challenges, the language mavens eventually found satisfaction when they entered a state of flow. It is only natural that they repeatedly sought to re-engage so that they could experience flow again. In a way, the primary goal for language mavens was to experience flow; their language development was almost secondary.

To a certain extent, it is spur-of-the-moment challenges that serve as entry points to *developing interests*. At one point, Andrew finally realized that he was going to live in China, he would have to move beyond simply teaching English and to learn to communicate fluently with his Chinese students and their parents. He merged his teaching skills in English with a new challenge—fluency in Chinese that would allow him to communicate unfettered with his students. Later, Andrew added an avid interest in Chinese culture and art.

If the learner can manage to merge current and developing interests into a single focus, flow becomes deeper and more sustained.

Rebecca also merged her interests in Spanish and education into a more complex activity where mastering Spanish and mastering theories in education became challenges of teaching Spanish as a second language at the university level. She discovered a connection between language learning and education that extended her experience of flow.

From a very young age, Emma had an interest in culture and history. As she developed an interest in American culture and history, she acquired skills in a parallel but related field: the English language. Emma merged her interest in American culture with mastery of the English language, thereby creating a more complex, nuanced perspective. Subsequently, she began to study Native American cultures and history, which led her to study the Cherokee and Lakota languages. Today, Emma finds it difficult to dissociate any aspect of language learning from culture (and vice versa).

In many ways, Scott's perspective of all languages as belonging to a single mega-system is the result of the merger of his training in engineering and his experience with learning languages. As an engineer would take apart a machine only to put it back together, Scott deconstructed languages, examined their internal workings, then reconstructed them.

Genevieve's knowledge of Latin was merged with her desire to master Arabic grammar. Beyond simply merging the two languages, she extracted the logic of an ancient language and applied it to a new one, going beyond the simple typological similarities the two languages share. In effect, Genevieve "cracked the code" of Latin and used it to help her unlock Arabic.

6. AN INTEREST IN LIFE PRECEDES AN INTEREST IN LANGUAGE

Among the language mavens, interest in language arose only subsequent to an interest in culture, traveling, living in another country, flirting, and playing around. In other words, language, itself, seldom provides the principal impetus for learning.

For Emma, culture was the gateway to language. Scott was interested in systems. Andrew wanted to travel. Rebecca wanted to have fun. Genevieve wanted to prove herself.

In *Arts as Experience*, American educator and philosopher John Dewey (1934) suggested that "completeness" is only possible with "a true experience." With a true experience, "every successive part flows freely, without seam and without unfilled blanks, into what ensues" (p. 206). Dewey saw a universality in true experience, "a single quality that pervades the entire experience in spite of the variation of its constituent parts" (p. 206). If true experience sounds like flow and feels like flow, it probably is flow.

7. THERE IS NO SINGLE PATH TO FLUENCY

All five language mavens personalized their study of the TL to fit their learning preferences and to maximize their language intake. The idea of scaffolding, of "taking it to the next step" is popular in the research literature of SLA.

While SLA theories often suggest that the teacher or the nature of the content should dictate "the next step," the research conducted for this book suggests that it is the learner, under the supervision of an expert (usually a teacher), who should decide the next step (McLaughlin, 1978). The process of ongoing self-examination teaches language learners how to set goals appropriate to their fluctuating levels of proficiency (Mirlohi, Egbert & Ghonsooly, 2011).

Scott's and Genevieve's approaches were systematic, while Emma's orientation was social. Andrew used highly behavioristic tactics to learn Chinese, while Rebecca tended to be spontaneous and contingent in learning Spanish. While individual approaches may have differed, each language maven was absolutely autonomous and gloriously idiosyncratic in the pursuit of the TL.

8. FLOW IS SUBJECTIVE

Flow is a perpetual circle in which the language learner continually moves. Performing well in an activity can increase interest, and increased interest tends to enhance the quality of the performance. The dialectical relationship between the individual and the outside world can result in learning when something old is connected with something new.

A constant negotiation occurs among learning, goals, the lived experience, and perception of the self. Performing well in an activity, such as language learning, depends on a convergence of factors. Positive experiences with language can lead to a state of flow and experiencing flow piques the desire for more frequent, positive experiences with language. Being good at language learning can make for an enjoyable experience, and having an enjoyable language experience can enhance language intake, that is to say, the rate and quality of acquisition.

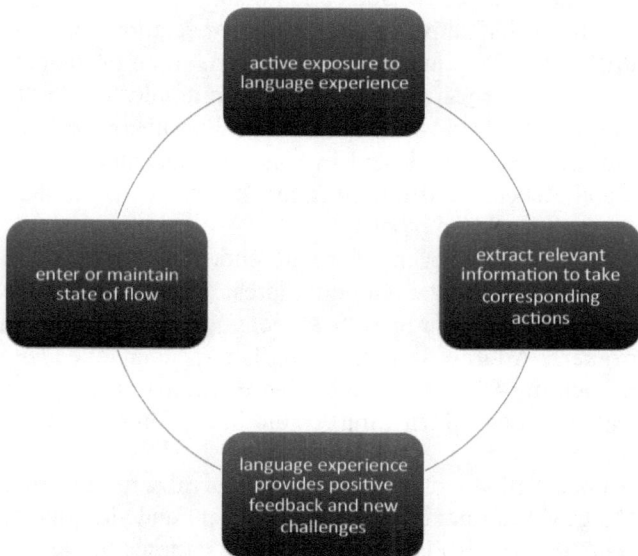

Figure C1. Language experience and flow.

To achieve flow, a person cannot sit on the sideline; he/she must be *actively engaged in the experience*. Being active means having the capacity to extract relevant information from the experience so that future challenges will match current skills. If challenges are well calibrated, the language learner will experience success, which reinforces the state of flow. In Figure C1, "state of flow" and "taking corresponding actions" are mechanisms that intervene inside the mind.

However, real experiences occur outside of the mind. Language mavens had no way of controlling their real, day-to-day interactions with the world, but they exhibited great control over their response to it. Indeed, all language mavens developed highly personalized, highly individualized responses to the environment.

Experience is not a factor, but a vector of flow. Two language learners can be exposed to the same experience, but the linguistic intake may be completely different for each person. Experience is the means to the end of language mastery, but the mind is both cause and effect.

Flow starts and ends in the mind as it attempts to subjectively mediate experience. For example, a language learner may be satisfied with a current level of proficiency in the language, although he/she may be far less proficient than another language learner who has higher aspirations and less self-satisfaction. Recall that Rebecca never considered pursuing any goal other than speaking "like a Castillian." The wide disparity in self-satisfaction among language learners makes one wonder about the extent to which linguistic knowledge is subjective and conditional.

Individuals have distinctive talents, their expectations are variable, and they hold different conceptions of what it means to be proficient in the TL. For some, proficiency means the ability to communicate and "get around" when traveling as a tourist in a foreign country. For others, proficiency means being able to seamlessly work and live in a foreign land. Emma, Andrew, Genevieve, and Rebecca did not consider themselves proficient until they were able to teach the TL to others.

Emma, a native speaker of French, ended up teaching English to international students in the United States. Rebecca, a native English speaker taught Spanish to university students, many of whom were native Spanish speakers. Andrew, a native English speaker, ended up teaching Chinese and helping Chinese students learn English. Genevieve, a native English speaker, ended up teaching Arabic in the United States and in the Middle East.

Scott was not satisfied with placing out of several semesters of Spanish, so he decided to travel to Spain to perfect his accent and significantly increase his facility with the Spanish language. When he returned to the United States, his proficiency was equal to some faculty in the Spanish Department at his university.

Differences in goals reflect, to an extent, differences in perceptions of anticipated uses of language. Teachers of languages at the secondary and post-secondary levels would do well to consider students' manifold motivations for studying a language (Schmidt, Boraie, & Kassabgy, 1996). Every student does not want to become bilingual, but every student can benefit by learning how to exert at least a little control over what is learned and how it is learned. The problem is that most language courses value knowledge of a predetermined curriculum over real learning because it is easier to measure. Real learning is fluctuating, overlapping, messy, and difficult to measure. Test scores provide neat, instant assessments, even if they indicate little about genuine language proficiency.

9. FLOW AMPLIFIES LANGUAGE LEARNING

A common feature among successful language learners is the ability to reflect on current strengths and weaknesses and to make informed decisions that lead to increasingly effective learning. The ability to self-monitor was paramount in the lives of each of the language mavens highlighted in this book.

A person in a state of flow has a heightened awareness, an effortless intensity, and an unflappable drive to succeed. A person who experiences flow in five minutes of learning a language may advance farther than a peer who goes through the routine of years of introductory courses and stacks of self-help books. A person who can tap into flow gains access to an instantaneous language learning amplifier.

Although some language courses already emphasize the importance of reflection (through portfolios, for example), it would be useful to ponder what a language curriculum that focuses on promoting flow experiences might look like. At a minimum, students would benefit dramatically from learning to identify strengths, to recognize weaknesses, and to devise plans of action to achieve desired goals.

Sigmund Freud's approach to the pleasure principle does not explain life's purpose, but it provides a frame for understanding human behavior. The pleasure principle does not explain what we should do, but who we are. Humans are prewired to seek pleasure and to avoid pain. Using the pleasure-seeking force in language classes or using it more seriously as the center of teaching would transform student perceptions of learning and extend learning well beyond the classroom walls. Enjoyment is possible through the subjective assessment of experience.

Language, Power, and the Quality of Life

Language is power and this power is determinant in the quest to comprehend reality, to understand the self, and to flourish in the environment in which you happen to be living.

All humans are unfinished, in a constant state of becoming. One way to view a human life is to think of it as the sum of experiences. If experiences are central to the quality of life, then by improving experience, the quality of life can be enhanced.

Yet, the quality of experience within a language classroom receives scant attention in the research literature, in institutions of learning, or in think tanks. Instead, the thrust in language learning for the past fifty years has been on standards, benchmarks, theory, and technical assessment, none of which contributes much to the quality of learning or the quality of life.

In most language classrooms today, instructors begin with an assault of drills and worksheets. The emphasis is on correctness and understanding new structures—sentences, vocabulary, pronunciation, writing rules, and tenses.

The instructor is responsible for determining what is to be learned, when it is to be learned, and how it is to be learned. The results of this research in to high-performing language mavens suggests that this approach is, at best, ineffective and, at worst, an impediment and a disincentive to real language learning.

All five language mavens began learning the language by playing with it. They tried out accents, made-up words, made incorrect conclusions, took innumerable wrong turns, and tried to be creative within the context of the language they understood. They had fun and they kept progressing, always setting their goals just a little higher than their current level of competence.

Their learning was both intensively private and purposefully social. Once they achieved a basic competence with language, they eagerly embraced drills and worksheets because they understood their particular weaknesses and used the drills and worksheets to specifically address them. Surprisingly, the relatively short period of intensive self-study was crucial in pushing the language mavens over the top and into fluency.

In the context of language acquisition, when a learner discovers a way to connect life choices to specific goals, then subsequently finds enjoyment in the pursuit of the goal, flow becomes possible.

As Csikszentmihalyi (2014) found repeatedly in his research, it is not the length of a life that matters, but what has been accomplished over the course of a life. In general, the higher the incidence of flow, the better the life. The difference in a life redolent with flow and one without flow is the difference between making a living and making a life.

References

Azizi, Z., & Ghonsooly, B. (2015). Exploring flow theory in TOEFL texts: Expository and argumentative genre. *Journal of Language Teaching & Research, 6*(1), 210–215.
Baines, L., & Yasuda, M. (2015). The high-achieving educational system of Japan. In Morgan, H., & Barry, C. (Eds.), *The world leaders in education: Lessons from the successes and drawbacks of their methods*, (pp. 61–78). New York, NY: Peter Lang.
Bar-Eli, M., & Azar, O. (2009). Penalty kicks in soccer: An empirical analysis of shooting strategies and goalkeepers' preferences. *Soccer & Society, 10*(2), 183–191.
Banks, J. A. (2004). Teaching for social justice, diversity and citizenship in a global world. *The Educational Forum, 68*(4), 296–305.
Birdsong, D. (1999). Whys and why nots of the Critical Period Hypothesis for second language acquisition. In D. Birdsong (Ed.) *Second language acquisition and the Critical Period Hypothesis* (pp. 1-21). Mahwah, NJ: Lawrence Erlbaum Publishers.
Bono, M., & Stratilaki, S. (2009). The m-factor a bilingual asset for plurilinguals? *International Journal of Multilingualism, 6*(2), 207–227.
Bouchentouf, A. (2006). *Arabic for dummies*. Hoboken, NJ: Wiley.
Caillois, R. (1961). *Man, play, and games*. Urbana, IL: University of Illinois Press.
Cenoz, J., Hufeisen B., & Jessner U., (2003). *The multilingual lexicon*, Dordrecht, The Netherlands: Kluwer Academic.
Cenoz, J. (2005). Review of 'Bilingualism: Beyond basic principles'. *Studies in Second Language Acquisition, 27*(1), 115–116.
Chomsky, N., & Skinner, B. (1959). Verbal behavior. *Language, 35*(1), 26.
Christoffels, I., Haan, A., Steenbergen, L., Wildenberg, W., & Colzato, L. (2015). Two is better than one: bilingual education promotes the flexible mind. *Psychological Research, 79*(3), 371–379.
Compton, W. (2005). *An introduction to positive psychology*. Belmont, CA: Thomson/Wadsworth.
Creswell, J. (2007). *Qualitative inquiry & research design: Choosing among five approaches*. Thousand Oaks, CA: SAGE Publications.

Csikszentmihalyi, M. (1990). *Flow: The psychology of optimal experience*. New York, NY: Harper & Row.

Csikszentmihalyi, M. (2014). Applications of flow in human development and education: The collected works of Mihaly Csikszentmihalyi. New York: Springer.

Deutscher, G. (2005). *The unfolding of language*. New York: Holt.

Dewey, J. (1902). *The child and the curriculum*. Chicago, IL: University of Chicago Press.

Dewey, J. (1934). *Art as experience*. New York, NY: Minton, Balch & Company.

Diamond, J. (2010). The benefits of multilingualism. *Science, 330*(6002), 332–333.

Diamond, M. (1988). *Enriching heredity*. New York, NY: Free Press.

Durkheim, E. (1951). *Suicide*. New York, NY: The Free Press.

Egbert, J. (2004). A study of flow theory in the foreign language classroom. *Canadian Modern Language Review, 60*(5), 549–585.

Fan, S., Liberman, Z., Keysar, B., & Kinzler, K. (2015). The exposure advantage: Early exposure to a multilingual environment promotes effective communication. *Psychological Science, 26*(7), 1090–1097.

Friedman, A. (2015). America's lacking language skills. *The Atlantic*. http://www.theatlantic.com/education/archive/2015/05/filling-americas-language-education-potholes/392876/.

Gardner, H. (1983). *Frames of mind*. New York, NY: Basic Books.

Gellner, E., & Russell, B. (1959). *Words and things: A critical account of linguistic philosophy and a study in ideology*. London, UK: V. Gollancz.

Gobel, P., & Mori, S. (2007). Success and failure in the EFL classroom: Exploring students' attributional beliefs in language learning. *EUROSLA Yearbook 7*(1), 149–169.

Falk, Y., & Bardel, C. (2011). Object pronouns in German L3 syntax: Evidence for the L2 status factor. *Second Language Research, 27*(1), 59–82.

Freire, P. (1970). *Pedagogy of the oppressed*. New York, NY: Herder and Herder.

Guillot, M. (1999). *Fluency and its teaching*. Clevedon, UK: Multilingual Matters.

Hafsa R., Umme H., Amara A., Adeeba A., & Shamsa K. (2014). Strategy inventory for language learning. *European Journal of Psychological Research, 1*(1). Retrieved from http://www.idpublications.org/wp-content/uploads/2014/11/Strategy.pdf.

Harley, T. (2008). *The psychology of language: From data to theory*, New York, NY: Psychology Press.

Horwitz, E. (2001). Language anxiety and achievement. *Annual Review of Applied Linguistics 21*, 112–126.

Jessner, U. (2003). The nature of cross-linguistic interaction in the multilingual system. In J. Cenoz, B. Hufeisen, & U. Jessner (Eds.), *The multilingual lexicon*, (pp. 45–55). New York, NY: Kluwer Academic Publishers.

Kantor, J. (1936). *An objective psychology of grammar*. Bloomington, IN: Indiana University.

Kellerman, E. (1986). *Crosslinguistic influence in second language acquisition*. New York, NY: Pergamon Institute of English.

Klabbers, J. (2000). Learning as acquisition and learning as interaction. *Simulation & Gaming, 31*(3), 380–406.

Kormos, J. (2006). *Speech production and second language acquisition*. New York, NY: Routledge.

Krashen, S. (1977). Some issues relating to the monitor model. In H. Brown, C. Yorio, & R. Crymes (Eds.), *Teaching and learning English as a second language: Trends in research and practice*, (pp. 144–158). Washington, DC: Teachers of Speakers of Other Languages.

Krashen, S. (1976). Formal and informal linguistic environments in language acquisition and language learning. *TESOL Quarterly, 10*(2), 157.

Lado, R. (1957). *Linguistics across cultures: Applied linguistics for language teachers*. Ann Arbor, MI: University of Michigan Press.

Lewis, B. (2014). *Fluent in 3 months: How anyone at any age can learn to speak any language from anywhere in the world*. New York, NY: Harperone.

Lightbown, P., & Spada, N. (2006). *How languages are learned*. Oxford, UK: Oxford University Press.

Lindqvist, C. (2009). The use of the L1 and the L2 in French L3: Examining Crosslinguistic lexemes in multilingual learners' oral production. *International Journal of Multilingualism, 6*(3), 281–297.

Martin, B. (2012). Coloured language: identity perception of children in bilingual programmes. *Language Awareness, 21*(1/2), 33–56.

Massimini, F., Csikszentmihalyi, M., & Massimo, C. (1987). The monitoring of optimal experience: A tool for psychiatric rehabilitation. *The Journal of Nervous and Mental Disease, 175*(9), 545–549.

McLaughlin, B. (1978). The monitor model: Some methodological considerations. *Language Learning 28*(2). 309–332.

Meijer, G., & Muysken, P. (1977). On the beginnings of pidgin and creole studies: Schuchardt and Hesseling. In A. Valdman, *Pidgin and creole linguistics*, (pp. 21–45). Bloomington, IN: Indiana University Press.

Merriam, S. (2009). *Qualitative research: A guide to design and implementation*. San Francisco: Jossey-Bass.

Mirlohi, M., Egbert, J., & Ghonsooly, B. (2011). Flow in translation: Exploring optimal experience for translation trainees. *Target: International Journal of Translation Studies, 23*(2), 251–271.

Muñoz, C. (2006). *Age and the rate of foreign language learning*. Clevedon, UK: Multilingual Matters.

Nicholson, N. (2014). *How to learn any language in a few months while enjoying yourself: 45 proven tips for language learners*. Amazon.com: Self-published book.

Oakfield, P. (2016). *How I learned to speak Spanish Fluently in three months: Discover how you can conquer Spanish easily the same*. Amazon.com: Self-published book.

Odlin, T. (1989). *Language transfer: Cross-linguistic influence in language learning*. Cambridge, UK: Cambridge University Press.

Ogbu, J. (1992). Understanding cultural diversity and learning. *Educational Researcher, 21*(8), 5–14.

Olsen, R. K., Pangelinan, M. M., Bogulski, C., Chakravarty, M. M., Luk, G., Grady, C. L., & Bialystok, E. (2015). The effect of lifelong bilingualism on regional grey and white matter volume. *Brain Research, 1612*, 128–139.

Ortega, L. (2009) *Understanding second language acquisition*. London, UK: Hodder Education.
Parker, P. (2009). *Second language acquisition: Webster's timeline history, 1966-2007*. San Diego, CA: ICON Group International.
Patton, M. (2002). *Qualitative research and evaluation methods*. Thousand Oaks, CA: SAGE Publications.
Penn, N. (2016). *How to learn a foreign language in four months: Proven methods for fluency*. Amazon.com: Self publication.
Piaget, Jean. (1959). *The language and thought of the child*. New York, NY: Humanities Press.
Poarch, G. J., & van Hell, J. G. (2012). Executive functions and inhibitory control in multilingual children: Evidence from second-language learners, bilinguals, and trilinguals. *Journal of Experimental Child Psychology, 113*(4), 535–551.
Pribaum, K. (1991). *Brain and perception*. Hillsdale, NJ: Lawrence Erlbaum.
Riggenbach, H. (2000). *Perspectives on fluency*. Ann Arbor, MI: University of Michigan.
Ringbom, H. (1987). *The role of the first language in foreign language learning*. Clevedon, UK: Multilingual Matters.
Rothman, J. (2011). L3 syntactic transfer selectivity and typological determinacy: The typological primacy model. *Second Language Research, 27*(1), 107–127.
Roy, D. (1960). Banana time: Job satisfaction and informal interaction. *Human Organization, 18*(4), 158–168.
Rubin, J. (1975). What the "good language learner" can teach us. *TESOL Quarterly, 9*(1), 41.
Saiz, A., & Zoido, E. (2005). Listening to what the world says: Bilingualism and earnings in the United States. *The Review of Economics and Statistics, 87*(3), 523–538.
Schiro, M. (2013). *Curriculum theory: Conflicting visions and enduring concerns*. Thousand Oaks, CA: SAGE Publications.
Schmidt, R., Boraie, D., & Kassabgy, O. (1996). Foreign language motivation: Internal structure and external connections. In R. Oxford (Ed.), *Language learning motivation: Pathways to the new century*, (pp. 9–56). Manoa, Hawai'i: University of Hawai'i Press.
Schmidt, R., & Savage, W. (1992). Challenge, skill, and motivation. *PASAA, 22*, 14–28.
Schmidt, R. (1992). Psychological mechanisms underlying second language fluency. *Studies in Second Language Acquisition, 14*(4), 357–385.
Schmidt N. (2002). *An introduction to applied linguistics*. Oxford, UK: Oxford University Press.
Schram, T. (2003). *Conceptualizing qualitative inquiry: Mindwork for fieldwork in education and the social sciences*. Upper Saddle River, NJ: Merrill/Prentice Hall.
Schwartz, C. (2011). Why It's Smart to Be Bilingual. *Newsweek, 158*(7), 26.
Segalowitz, N. (2010). *Cognitive bases of second language fluency*. New York, NY: Routledge.
Seligman, M. (2002). *Authentic happiness*. New York, NY: Atria Books.

Selinker, L. (1972). Interlanguage. *International Review of Applied Linguistics, 10*, 209–241.

Sentürk, B. (2012). Teachers' and students' perceptions of flow in speaking activities. *International Journal of Management Economics & Business/Uluslararasi Yönetim Iktisat Ve Isletme Dergisi, 8*(16), 283–306.

Sahinkarakas, S. (2011). Young students' success and failure attributions in language learning. *Social Behavior & Personality: An International Journal, 39*(7), 879–885.

Simsek, S. (2006). *Third language acquisition: Turkish-German bilingual students acquisition of English word order in a German educational setting*. Münster, Germany: Waxmann Verlag GmbH.

Singleton, D. (1987). Mother and other tongue influence on learner French: A case study. *Studies in Second Language Acquisition, 9*(3), 327–346.

Swain, M. (2005). The output hypothesis: Theory and research. In E. Hinkel (Ed.), *Handbook of research in second language teaching and learning*, (pp. 471–483). Mahwah, NJ: Lawrence Erlbaum.

Tardy, C., & Snyder, B. (2004). 'That's why I do it': Flow and EFL teachers' practices. *ELT Journal, 58*(2), 118–128.

Vygotsky. L. (1978). *Mind in society*. Cambridge, MA: Harvard University Press.

Westly, E. (2011). The bilingual advantage. *Scientific American Mind, 22*(3), 38–41.

Williams, S., & Hammarberg, B. (1998). *Language switches in L3 production: Implications for a polyglot speaking model. Applied Linguistics,19*(3), 295–333.

Wyner, G. (2014). *Fluent gorever: How to learn any language fast and never forget it*. New York, NY: Harmony Books.

Xiaowei, G. (2013). A study on Flow Theory and translation teaching in China's EFL class. *Journal of Language Teaching & Research, 4*(4), 785–790.

About the Authors

Born and raised in France, **Noumane Rahouti** is a second generation immigrant from Morocco. He grew up speaking French and Berber. He obtained a Ph.D. in Education and Second Language Acquisition from the University of Oklahoma where he also taught English as a Second Language and Spanish. He also accumulated experience teaching in England, France, and Saudi Arabia. He dedicated his research to two major fields, Second Language Acquisition and the Sociology of Minorities in France. He is now a Lecturer at the University of Central Florida, Orlando, FL, USA.

Lawrence Baines is an Associate Dean and Professor of English Education at The University of Oklahoma. His website is www.lawrencebaines.com.

www.ingramcontent.com/pod-product-compliance
Lightning Source LLC
Chambersburg PA
CBHW020752230426
43665CB00009B/569